DOG
SOLDIERS

Also by Isabel George

Buster: The Dog Who Saved a Thousand Lives
Murphy the Hero Donkey
The 9/11 Dogs
Warrior
The Dog that Saved My Life
Beyond the Call of Duty

ISABEL GEORGE

DOG SOLDIERS

LOVE, LOYALTY AND SACRIFICE ON THE FRONT LINE

HarperElement
An imprint of HarperCollins*Publishers*
1 London Bridge Street
London SE1 9GF

www.harpercollins.co.uk

First published by HarperElement 2016

1 3 5 7 9 10 8 6 4 2

© Isabel George 2016

Isabel George asserts the moral right to be
identified as the author of this work

A catalogue record of this book is
available from the British Library

ISBN 978-0-00-814806-5

Printed and bound in Great Britain by
Clays Ltd, St Ives plc

MIX
Paper from
responsible sources
FSC™ C007454

FSC™ is a non-profit international organisation established to promote
the responsible management of the world's forests. Products carrying the
FSC label are independently certified to assure consumers that they come
from forests that are managed to meet the social, economic and
ecological needs of present and future generations,
and other controlled sources.

Find out more about HarperCollins and the environment at
www.harpercollins.co.uk/green

Northern Ireland border, Clogher, County Tyrone, 23 July 1973
Corporal Bryan Criddle RAVC was injured when an IRA bomb, hidden in a milk churn, was detonated remotely. He died due to head injuries four days later. His dog, Jason, was blown 30 feet in the air but survived.

Northern Ireland, Kilkeel, 28 May 1986
Corporal Brian Brown QGM from Ballynahinch was a member of 3 UDR (Ulster Defence Regiment) and had been awarded the Queen's Gallantry Medal for his service in Northern Ireland. He lost his life on 28 May 1986 when a bomb exploded at a garage in Kilkeel. Oliver, his search dog, was also killed in the blast. The ashes of the faithful Yellow Labrador were buried with his master.

Northern Ireland, Crossmaglen, 21 May 1988
Corporal Derek Hayes of the Royal Pioneer Corps died with his Army search dog, Ben, when an IRA booby trap bomb exploded. Cpl Hayes and Ben were on patrol in Crossmaglen when they were asked to investigate a partly hidden box in a ditch but as they approached the device exploded, killing them both. The ashes of the faithful Yellow Labrador were buried alongside the soldier.

Northern Ireland, Belfast, 25 May 1991
Corporal Terry 'Geordie' O'Neill was the victim of a 'coffee-jar' bomb (Semtex, nails, bolts and ball bearings). He was killed instantly. Darren 'Swifty' Swift, his fellow handler, standing alongside him, lost both legs in the attack, which took place as the two soldiers exercised their dogs in the yard of the Army Dog Unit. Several dogs were injured in the blast, including Geordie's dog, Blue, and Swifty's dog, Troy.

Four dog soldiers lost their lives during The Troubles in Northern Ireland, between 1973 and 1991. The conflict in Afghanistan was to claim the next man and dog.

Contents

Introduction

As you made your way to the kennels at Camp Bastion it's said you could hear, from metres away, the dogs preparing their noisy welcome. Your walk would take you past innumerable dust-covered vehicles, and around you men and women in desert fatigues moved with constant purpose as life played out on the British Forces base in Afghanistan.

In among these scenes of everyday life stood memorials to the fallen – like markers among the living. Sand-coloured walls of Remembrance and glistening brass crosses rose defiant against the Afghan sky, bearing the names of the mighty and the brave: the men, women and dogs killed in action since the conflict began in 2001.

The memorial to the fallen dog soldiers wasn't easy to miss: it wasn't meant to be. And it wasn't hewn from traditional cold stone or rock. The lovingly carved wooden paw linked with metal chains was created by members of the RAVC (Royal Army Veterinary

Corps) in honour of their own. It bore the names of two brave young soldiers and their loyal bomb dogs: Lance Corporal Kenneth Rowe and his dog Sasha, and Lance Corporal Liam Tasker and his dog Theo.

The men and their dogs died in the line of fire. The RAVC lost two men and dogs, and two mothers lost their sons.

The two boys grew up with a love of animals – especially dogs – and a desire to not just do a job but enjoy their chosen career. To them, life was too precious to waste on doing something that meant nothing. They were lucky, as they both had the support of their families, and when the RAVC became their second home it was a choice their mothers understood. The love of dogs was in their blood, an echo from childhood, and it had found its way through again. And for both mothers there was one massive comfort: their sons would never be lonely with a dog at their side.

Kenneth and Liam didn't need to be told that working with dogs is never a walk in the park, but for them the job was a joy. The series of protection dogs, and then the bomb dogs, all left their mark – some more permanent than others. In whatever discipline they were working both men stood out from the pack as natural handlers. Their skills were noted by their superiors and they were the ones to watch as rising stars. Both had a way with dogs and were good with people, and, more than that, they were dedicated to the Corps and all it stood for.

No one could have been more proud of their sons than Lyn Rowe and Jane Duffy. To see their boys happy and doing the job they loved was about as much as a mum could wish for. The two young men had found their true vocation. Now all their mothers could do was sit back and watch their sons' lives play out.

A soldier signs up to serve their country, every family knows that, and for these two young military dog handlers the call came to deploy to Afghanistan. For Kenneth and Liam Operation Herrick meant working on the front line, every second putting their life on the line and in the care of the dog at their side. For the family serving at home it meant reliance on letters, emails and the odd phone call. These they clung to for confirmation that their loved one was still alive.

But for Lyn and Jane the flurry of blueys, care parcels, dog treats and crossing dates on the calendar suddenly came to an end. Lance Corporal Kenneth Rowe and military working dog Sasha were killed in action on 24 July 2008. Lance Corporal Liam Tasker was killed in action on 1 March 2011 and his military working dog Theo died of a seizure just hours later.

Their names appear together on the memorial to Afghanistan's fallen dog soldiers. Soldiers first, dog lovers always. Soldier and dog bound for life and beyond.

Mothers, Lyn and Jane, still feel the loss and miss the life occupied by their brave boys, but they are proud of their sons and that they did their job, served their country and made the ultimate sacrifice. Knowing they didn't die alone, their tears are broken with some small comfort that their sons fell with their best friend at their side.

Maybe the warm desert air still echoes with the names of these young men and their dogs, Sasha and Theo, and their ghosts still drift along the ripples in the sand side by side as they lived and died so far from home.

Isabel George, September 2015

Chapter 1

Please God,
look after him …

Lyn Rowe stirred to the glare of headlights at the bedroom window. Transfixed by the light and the silence she flinched at the 'clunk' of the car door and the tip-tap of footsteps on the drive, but in that moment Lyn already knew this wasn't the neighbours returning late or a stranger who had taken a wrong turning.

Lyn was halfway down the stairs when she heard the doorbell. Caught in a frightening wave of certainty she had no doubt that the dark-suited figure standing at her front door was the messenger she prayed would never visit her family.

'Mrs Rowe? Can I come in please?'

The man held his ID card against the window by the door.

'No, you can't come in!' Lyn found her voice as she felt her husband's arm around her. 'I can't let you in because I know what you're going to tell me.'

K, the family's dog, was barking like mad as the caller tried again: 'I need to speak to you, Mrs Rowe.'

All five foot two inches of Lyn Rowe was now barring the door. 'Now why would I let you into my house when I know what you are going to say to us? No, go away!'

Ken Rowe stepped forward, standing tall between his wife and the door.

'Mr Rowe,' the messenger persisted, 'can you please ask your wife to open the door?'

LYN

We must have stood in the hall a good few minutes looking through the glass porch at the man waiting. I knew that if I let him into our home my world would change and I was prepared to stand there forever if it meant never having to hear the words he had come to say.

All the time we stood there I felt as if my feet had been bolted to the floor, but the moment Ken pulled me closer I knew the wait was over. He loosened his grip on my arm and leant out to open the door.

'Mr and Mrs Rowe, I'm sorry for the early hour but I need to speak with you. Can I come in?'

I didn't have a chance to say no again as the man took advantage of the open door, as I knew he would. I couldn't move. I was transfixed by his boots as he wiped them on the mat and Ken showed him into the lounge.

I only remember flashes of what happened next but I know he asked us to sit down, but I took the news standing up.

'We've received news that concerns your son, Kenneth. He was on duty in Helmand Province with B Company 2nd Battalion Parachute Regiment (2 Para) when they came under heavy attack from a group of insurgents armed with rocket-propelled grenades. Kenneth took a direct hit and his dog, Sasha, too. They were killed instantly. They fell together, Mrs Rowe. Kenneth didn't die alone.'

A silence overpowered the room. The dog stopped barking.

There's still a sense of the surreal about that morning. It's not because of what was said to me, because I knew what that would be from the first flash of the car headlights, but maybe it's more to do with the short time it took for it to be explained. In less than an hour I had lost my son. He was 24 years old.

Kenneth (I always call him Kenneth as his father is Ken) was a soldier who loved dogs and died doing the job he loved. I knew that if there was any way by which he would have wanted to leave us forever it would have been doing his duty as a Military Working Dog handler. It was the job he wanted to do and the one he signed up for. And to have his search dog, Sasha, at his side at the end, well, maybe he would have been characteristically … proud. Proud to have been doing his duty to the last second of his life.

Of course, none of that came into my head that July morning in 2008. I've since been told that what happened next was done in shock and denial, and maybe that's right. One thing I'm sure of is that Kenneth would have been surprised if I had behaved in any other way.

'So how long do I have to tell the family?' I remember asking the man from the MoD. 'We have a large family and I want them to hear this news from me, not the BBC. How long?'

He told me we had until late morning, latest, as Kenneth's death would be announced on the BBC lunchtime news. And he needed a photograph of my son, if that was all right.

It was still only 3am but by then time was irrelevant. I am one of six children and Ken had his mother and two sisters to reach, so with nephews, nieces and cousins on top of that it was pretty much a race against time. He kindly asked if there was anything he could do to help. I hope he saw that I was already making a list in my head of people I needed to speak to, and as soon as he left I started transferring my thoughts to paper.

I decided it was too early to start calling people, even family – after all, it was the kind of news that could wait until everyone else's day had begun. Nothing was going to change the news or make it any better, but at least I could make a list of who needed to know. I decided that 6am would be a good time to start making the rounds. But what about work?

As Practice Manager for a large legal firm in Newcastle I always had plenty on my plate. All my friends and colleagues know I'm a workaholic, but at that particular time I was right in the middle of an audit that would achieve a European standard for all the offices in the firm. The audit was nearly over and there was no way I was going to walk out and let everyone down. I told myself that I was going to complete it and cope.

I filled two pages of A4 notepaper with instructions for the team. Every detail of all they had to do to complete the audit and achieve the accreditation was there. It was still only 5.30am but I decided that it was best to deliver the notes and the files I had with me to the office so they would be there when it opened. Ken drove while I thought back over what I'd written, but when we arrived I realised that I couldn't get into the main building without setting off the full alarm system. Thankfully I had access to the garage so we stacked the boxes of files in there and put the notes on top. I knew I could explain anything else when I phoned my boss later. That was work done. Sorted.

Now, my family.

It was still only 6.10am. Then it hit me, my beautiful girls. I had to tell them they had lost their brother. Dear God – was this some kind of nightmare?

When we arrived at Jennifer's house I sat in the car for a minute or so to get myself together before Ken took my hand to help me out of the car. I will never forget Jeni's face when she opened the door; she knew something was very wrong and I'm not sure that it really registered when I finally uttered the words: 'Kenneth's been killed ...'

She took the news reasonably well. Probably in shock, I realise that now. We hugged like we would never let each other go. Ken held us both. Our rock. Our protector. But even this was beyond him.

We couldn't bear to leave Jeni behind so she came with us to Stephanie's home, just a short distance away. It's still a comfort to know they live so close to each other and that morning I was especially relieved as Steph took it very badly. Kenneth was her big brother and watched over her. Yes, he could be more than over-protective, but it was all part of his love for his little sister. Now he was gone.

I hated seeing my girls in tears. I would have given anything to just get them together and hide away from the world, but the burden of having to reach the rest of the family within the next four hours was weighing heavy on me now.

I'm the second child in a family of six and I'm half Chinese. My father was in the Royal Signals and met my mother when he was stationed in Hong Kong. They met, fell in love, and when my father's tour of duty ended he brought his Chinese bride back to Newcastle. I'm sure it was quite a culture shock for her – 1950s Newcastle was dark and industrial and a far cry from the vibe and colour of Hong Kong. Nevertheless, despite the influences around her she brought up her family in line with her strong Chinese ethos. The family bond was close and unbreakable and family always came first.

In Chinese families you go by your number in the family: number 1 child, number 2 child, etc, and even then the boys take the lead followed by the girls. So, it was natural to me to put the number system into play when deciding who to inform first. My elder sister, Jann, took the news well, although she was clearly upset. My sister Lesley was inconsolable and crumpled on receiving the news. I said to her: 'Please don't do this to me!' I was finding it hard to keep myself together and strong enough to get around everyone so all we could do was bundle her into the car and take her with us.

The impact on my brothers, Martin and Gary, was excruciating to watch. They loved Kenneth like a son and now they had the pain of telling their own children that he had been killed.

There was only my 'baby sis' Michelle left to tell then, and I was dreading it. I was so glad that Lesley was with us and could help us to comfort her because as we stood together the grief was palpable. But I could not let it take me yet. My job wasn't finished.

Ken's mother was on holiday so his two sisters had the dreadful job of telling her when she returned. We did not want her holiday spoilt as she could not change anything – no one could.

At 9am on the dot I called my boss at work. 'Hi Stephen, it's Lyn. I've got some bad news. Kenneth has died. He's been killed in Afghanistan.' There was silence on the end of the phone and then he said: 'Oh my God. What are you doing ringing me?'

I remember telling him to please be quiet and I needed to talk to him about the audit. I also recall his reply: 'Forget the audit! What about you? I'm happy to cancel the audit. Just tell me what we can do to help you?' There was only one answer to that – carry on with the audit. I hadn't done all that work to have them pull out now, especially as I had spent over an hour sorting the files and the notes. It was still my responsibility and I was not going to be the excuse that let the whole team down. I made Stephen promise that it would go ahead.

Then everything went blank.

* * *

From the moment the messenger from the MoD left our home that morning I think the bulk of my sadness found a place to hide inside me. I couldn't give in to it until all the practical things had been ticked off the list.

I'm sure I listened to all the man had to say (though, for the life of me, I can't remember much at all). I'm sure I probably thanked him for coming and for his patience and for his offer of help and his advice. In the silent moments after Ken showed the man out I no doubt thought what a horrid job that must be to have to visit parents in the dead of night and give them the worst news they could ever imagine. I wondered how he must feel now, driving back to wherever. I'm sure he breathed a sigh of relief as soon as he sat back in the car and told himself that he never wanted to do that again – knowing that he would have to, sooner or later.

I didn't blame him – it wasn't his fault – but he had opened a portal direct to hell, and for me there was no way out.

I cried, of course I cried, but I didn't fall apart – not then.

The funny thing was, I had felt odd all that previous day.

I had been on day three of the four-day audit and I was driving back from the Carlisle office when I heard a loud 'boom'. I was on the A69 at about 5.30pm so I wondered if I had kicked something up off the road that had hit the car, or perhaps that someone behind me had experienced a tyre blow-out or a mechanical problem. I couldn't see anything and my car was still driving OK, so I carried on. I just wanted to get home.

It had been a long day and I blamed that for the 'low' feeling and whatever it was that was making me feel 'not right'. The journey had not been too painful but I was glad to swing the car onto the drive and turn off the ignition. Home.

Ken was already there, which meant the evening meal would be on the go and a pot of tea at the ready. That realisation would usually be enough to ease my stress level and calm me down but that odd feeling was still in the pit of my stomach and I didn't like it at all.

As I kicked off my shoes in the hall I noticed something that made me feel worse: the white orchid that Kenneth had given me for Mother's Day had dropped a bloom. Not only that but the leaves were turning brown and some had already fallen. I accept that house plants die and orchids are particularly fragile – I should know as I love them and had kept them for years – but the thing about this particular orchid was that it had flowered so well and for so long. Kenneth had had to give it to me well in advance of Mother's Day as he knew he would be in Afghanistan in March. Everyone who'd seen it had remarked on its beauty and staying power.

I stood looking at it for a few minutes and felt quite sick. I took it as a sign of change and from that moment I felt restless.

I was tired that night but I couldn't sleep. I should have been ready for bed and some good refreshing sleep but all I could manage was lots of tossing and turning. Even when I dozed off I was awake in minutes, with my head spinning.

It was then that I saw the headlights at the bedroom window.

'This is the lunchtime news from the BBC:
'The Army dog handler killed in Afghanistan on Thursday has been named by the Ministry of Defence. Lance Corporal Kenneth Michael Rowe, of the Royal Army Veterinary Corps, who was 24, and from Newcastle, had been due to leave the front line the day before he died. He and his explosives search dog, Sasha, died after coming under Taliban fire during a routine patrol in Helmand. Lance Corporal Rowe had asked not to leave on Wednesday as he worried about his base not having enough search cover. The death brings the total number of British service personnel who have died in Afghanistan to 112.

'Lance Corporal Rowe's commanding officer, Major Stuart McDonald, said, "This unselfish action epitomises his professionalism and dedication to his job. I feel lucky to have known him and gutted to have to say goodbye."

'Kenneth Rowe and his dog Sasha were the first Royal Army Veterinary Corps dog and handler to be killed in action since The Troubles in Northern Ireland.'

So it was real.

I remember, we were standing in the kitchen with my brother, Gary, when I heard Kenneth's name on the television. There on the screen was the photograph of my son in his dress uniform. The photograph that, until a few hours before, had been hanging, in its frame, on the stairs. My handsome son. My beautiful boy.

That was the moment when I let go.

If someone asked me to tell them exactly what happened next I would have only one answer – I've no idea.

I had motored through the previous ten hours on auto-pilot, with a huge heap of denial thrown in, but when reality was eventually allowed in it took over. My sister Lesley came over and decided I needed tranquillisers to calm me down, but I didn't want to leave the house and the medication couldn't be prescribed over the telephone so, bizarrely, I found myself sitting in the doctor's waiting room in floods of tears. There I was, patiently waiting for my appointment and wondering what on earth I was doing there!

I'm sure the pills worked, taking the edge off whatever I was feeling, but I don't think anything could have taken away the anger that rose inside me when the press started knocking on the door. Waves of well-meaning neighbours at the door was one thing, but having the media parked outside on the lawn was something else. We are very close and keep everything within our family unit – we solve our own problems together – but suddenly the BBC News had exposed our loss, our soft underbelly, and we felt vulnerable. Ken and my brothers dealt with the press on the doorstep. A simple 'leave us alone' seemed to work effectively, at least on the decent ones.

Me? I just wanted it all to go away.

The awful thing is, just hours before our nightmare began, Kenneth was supposed to be on his way home to us.

The day I drove to Carlisle for the audit Kenneth emailed me at 6am: 'Hi, Mam. Who will be picking me up and what time?' I remember saying: 'Don't worry about that, son, you just get yourself home. It'll be me or your dad. I'm off to work now so I'll ask your dad to call you back later to let you know who will be there for you.'

That was it. I had visions of Kenneth finishing his duties at Bastion then packing and getting ready to catch the next Helmand Taxi (as they called the Chinook) out to start his journey to RAF Brize Norton where the military aircraft landed and … home. Friday was to be the last day of my audit, which was great because, once I had thought about the timings, I knew that I would be able to be with Ken when he drove down to Brize to pick up Kenneth. I wanted to see our son so much.

This was July and I hadn't seen him since the Deployment Party in February. Kenneth had enjoyed being with his mates and his family and it was great to meet the people he would be spending the next few months with in Afghanistan. They would be his 'family' until he came home again and they had seemed a great bunch of lads.

I will never forget what Kenneth was wearing that night – a salmon-pink T-shirt. It wasn't my cup of tea and he probably knew that. It was funny to me because Kenneth was always so smart; he thought about everything he wore and his thick dark brown hair was always gelled into place. He had told me that a lot of his Army friends had thought he had Mediterranean blood but he always said he was proud to tell them that his dark hair and olive complexion were thanks to his half-Hong Kong Chinese mother. I liked that.

The morning after the party there he was at breakfast – in the same T-shirt. I had to ask him if he had anything else to wear, which he knew I would at some point. But of course he was travelling light and was meeting friends later so I understood when he said, 'Sorry, Mam, this is all I've got, but you won't forget it, will you?' It's true, that shirt made a lasting impression on me. I sometimes forgot that he was 24 years old, but then he was always ready to remind me that he was no longer my little boy.

It was one of those mornings when we knew we would have to say goodbye to Kenneth later and I was keen to have some breakfast with him before he announced that he needed to be somewhere else to meet his friends. 'What do you want for breakfast, son?' his dad asked, as he was probably ready for something himself. The expected answer came back: McDonald's.

It wouldn't have been everyone's choice but it was always going to be Kenneth's, especially as he knew he wouldn't be tasting anything like that for a few months. At breakfast I discovered that it's difficult to eat when your throat is so tight you can hardly breathe, and then all too soon the moment had come – breakfast was over and the goodbyes had to begin.

Kenneth hugged all the family, then his dad and then me.

'I love you, son,' I said. He hugged me back. 'I'll write as often as I can and send parcels. Let us know if you need anything,' I continued. He started to cry. 'Now stop it or you'll start me off,' I scolded him. His hug tightened.

'I just want you to know that I love you, Mam.'

I'm not sure if that last hug was tighter than normal or that's a trick my mind has played on my memory of that morning since then, but if I think about that moment I can still feel Kenneth's arms around me.

'Now just don't be stupid and volunteer for anything' I said. 'Promise me you won't volunteer and you won't put yourself up front. Promise me, Kenneth.'

I remember him walking away saying: 'Right, Mam. OK, Mam …' But as I watched him from behind I saw him drying tears, first with one hand then the next. My beautiful brown-eyed boy in his salmon-pink T-shirt.

It's my lasting memory of him.

Of course, after that our contact was down to the usual and very welcome flurry of 'blueys'. Those pale-blue airmail paper letters are still a lifeline in Forces' families. I'm sure none of us knows what we would do without them. The emails and the phone calls are great – as long as they can be sent and received. As Kenneth said when he was in Afghan, 'Emails … can't get them in the desert. Still waiting on that terminal you plug into the sand!'

Letters were always precious and there was a massive comfort in seeing a bluey drop onto the mat. Kenneth's spelling was atrocious and he knew it. But it didn't matter one bit because, to me, receiving a bluey meant he was alive, able to write a letter and thinking of home. Parcels and letters to Kenneth often arrived around five days after sending and some wandered around following 'the dog handler' as he moved between camps, including the main base, Camp Bastion, and the various Forward Operating Bases

(FOBs). But there was never any doubt that the post would be delivered to him somewhere and sometime.

Every letter was a window into our son's world in Afghanistan and every anecdote came with a handful of sand.

I remember in one of his letters he told his dad about how he had to 'dig in' to protect himself and the bomb dog he was working with then, Diesel, against yet another biting sandstorm. He had told us before how, after the blistering heat of the day, the storms blew in fiercely during the night '... *like a blanket of sand hitting you for about six hours non-stop. We woke up looking like something from f...ing Kentucky Fried Chicken!*'

Kenneth was deployed on Operation Herrick 8 in March 2008 and whenever I read and re-read the letters, just to have him with me for a second, I realised that while I was here missing him he was there but always reaching out to home. If there was one thing Kenneth always made sure of, wherever he was, it was that we had his address. There were few letters that didn't contain a shopping list but I soon realised that a shopping list was a way of guaranteeing that there would be a parcel to look forward to. Sweets, biscuits, baby wipes, boxers and ... socks. I have no idea how many pairs of socks I sent to Afghanistan but then I had no real idea how important something as simple as a pair of socks could be out there.

'Socks. Oh my God, socks. They are a f…ing life-saver, Mam. Pardon the language, like, but my feet might get some feeling in them now. Imagine 35–40 degree heat walking around the pissing desert for six hours at a time.

'Tell Dad I got to throw my first live grenade the other day. Mint! Absolutely mint! I'll tell you about it when I'm home. Ha! Ha! Ain't had chance to let my rifle do any work yet but hey there's 5½ months to go.'

Looking back, knowing what I know now, I still understand my son's excitement because this was what he wanted to do. This is what he had trained so hard for, and there he was, in his words, 'living the dream'. And of course the dream job came with a dog.

It must have been in his second bluey home that Kenneth told us that he had been taken off protection work and had, at last, been assigned an arms and explosives search (AES) dog called Diesel.

'I haven't got a complaint about him at all apart from he loves other dogs too much. I'll have to watch that when we're working coz the local dogs will kill him if he gets too close. What else can I tell you except, don't worry … If anything was to happen to me you would be notified quickly enough. They would either ring your mobile or home. Not going to happen.'

Every letter after that was signed off not just by Kenneth but with love from Diesel, too – never forgetting the mini paw print. My son was happy and so was

I because now, wherever he was, he would not be alone.

Through March and into April Kenneth was in Afghanistan but his letters betrayed that his mind was still at home. He had to post his mobile phone back to me and of course there was a bill to pay. I could tell that bit of admin was worrying him, and so for the same reason he authorised me to deal with all his post that came to him at our home. I didn't mind, after all, as there was little he could do about all that from where he was. Trying to deal with a call centre from the comfort of your own home is frustrating enough but it's near impossible when you have to book telephone and internet time at Camp Bastion on equipment that's shared with several hundred other people. Besides, I liked to feel needed. That was normal, as a mum.

I was already missing Kenneth's constant cries of, 'Mam, could you just ... Mam, while you're in town could you pick me up some ...' There was always something he wanted me to get for him, even when he was home.

I'm not just saying this because he was my son, but he was a good-looking boy and he liked to look smart even when he was in casual clothes, which included his beloved Newcastle United football shirt. Kenneth liked specific toiletries so his shopping list would be pretty detailed and he wouldn't be seen out of the house without hair gel. His sisters were always complaining that he spent too long in the bathroom and it was a family joke that if you didn't make it into the shower before Kenneth you would be waiting forever!

It was no surprise to any of us that his blueys almost always contained some kind of shopping list. It made me smile thinking of him sitting on his camp cot in the desert, paper resting on his knees – just as he did as a boy doing his homework – pen poised ready to scribble down all the things he had been saving in his head.

April 2008, his first bluey after just being posted to Camp Roberts at Kandahar Airfield said:

'*Hi Parents … How are we today? I've been good since the last time we spoke and fully integrated with my battle group. That sounds quite scary really, "battle group". Ha, ha. Me going into battle is probably never going to happen and I'll never get a chance to get some rounds off as the Platoon I'm with will do all that for me. It would be an experience, I reckon, and nice to see how I would cope with it after all the training. Be good to kick in and really enjoy it. Diesel is doing well. He's chasing flies at the moment in the living room at the kennels I'm staying at … My new address means you won't have to send stuff through Bastion anymore so you can get things to me a lot easier.*

'*I have a list of things needed or liked. Not necessarily to be sent all at once … and I've asked Jeni to send some stuff so if you can tie in with her plz ... at least I will have them for when I get back from the job I'm going on. So, watch, trainer socks, baby wipes, photos of the family, Bonjela, something to cut my nails with other than my bayonet, under crackers (pants) and dog treats and toys for Diesel – oh, and a digital camera (there was one in Argos quite cheap). There are cameras out here but they are six megapixel shite ... and the phone I sent back to you is bloody five million pixels. I wanted a better one to keep pictures of my experiences here. I should have thought about it long before this, like.'*

While his dad got questions about the car and if it had been fixed yet, and the state of Newcastle United, Kenneth made sure his girls did his shopping! He knew we would run around and made sure there was always one parcel on its way and another being made up. We soon got used to the delay in his requests coming in, the parcel leaving home and arriving with him. Numbering the parcels helped, too, so he knew what to expect in each and which email or letter it corresponded with. It was a bit of a science, really, and certainly there was nothing random about it.

Of course, there was the odd challenge, like the time he asked for Drumstick lollies in a bluey on 10 April:

'Thanks again for the watch and the socks. Guys are already sick of the T-shirt and me getting news of Newcastle victories. It's great! Oh, Mam, can you find

me some Drumstick lollies? I had a craving for them along with some malted milk biscuits. Ahhh, I know it's hard maybe to do but a "brew" kit – some real teabags. Sugar I'll be able to steal and we've got dried milk but a packet of real teabags plz. I miss a good brew. Oh well, speak again soon. All my love as always, Ken xxx and Diesel xxx'

Sometimes, in those early days of Kenneth being in Afghanistan I forgot that I was sending this stuff into temperatures of 30 to 40 degrees plus. I was over the moon to find Drumstick lollies aplenty in our local shop. As I grabbed a handful out of the box on the counter I imagined the broad grin that would appear on my son's face when he opened the envelope and there they would be, along with his requested biscuits, sports mags and back copies of the *Newcastle Chronicle*, plus the little surprises that Jeni and Steph had prepped for him. Envelope sealed and addressed to Lance Corporal Kenneth Rowe, Dog Handler, Op Herrick 8, I felt pure joy as the woman at the post office took it from me. To me, it was already on its way.

Then came the 'thank you' bluey:

'Hi Mam, Received your parcel today which was a nice touch – everything was crushed and melted, like. The Drumstick lollies were open and had leaked onto the newspapers with the melted chocolate off the biscuits! ... Never mind ... I've been putting some weight back on but just on my stomach ... not good ...

I will have to go running when I get home. You get any passes for the gym?'

I tried a second time with the lollies and all landed successfully – wrapped and intact. Kenneth must have decided to share them out or the opening of his parcel had attracted a crowd because he wrote to say: *'… can't believe how much a small thing like a Drumstick lolly can put such big smiles on the faces of four grown men!'* I like to think of him sitting eating the lollies – bought in a little shop in Newcastle – with his mates in the dust of Afghanistan.

He always said the parcels were a massive boost to morale and there was always huge excitement when the post arrived – it didn't matter whose post. The contents of letters and parcels were always likely to be a source of comfort, amusement, relief, joy and some-times ridicule from their mates. Kenneth's parcels always had to have that extra something – for the dog. Non-melting, of course.

After that I was much more careful about wrapping each item before adding them to his parcels. Sending things when he was based in Northern Ireland had been much easier – searing heat was never likely to be a problem there, although drowning would have been no surprise as every letter and phone call featured a rain report. From March to April 2008, almost every letter from Kenneth featured the weather, but it was all about heat and dust, rain and sand.

At first the sunshine was a novelty and there were plenty of 'no time to sunbathe' jokes and tales of sunscreen shortages. Kenneth liked the sun and he had inherited my olive skin but the Afghan heat was too intense even for him. Soon it began to affect everything from his sleep to his general morale. By the end of April he was wishing for snow and when the rain came he wanted it to go away. Kenneth was never shy of a good moan, and I'm sure his Army mates were used to it, too, but once he had said his piece he admitted he felt better: 'rant over'.

Kenneth worried about Diesel, too. He always told us how well his dog was working, but shelter and rest were important and Kenneth's Bergen was always packed with food, treats and a blanket for Diesel. Whatever the weather had to offer, Diesel would be OK. If Kenneth had to dig in for shelter he dug a man-and-Labrador-sized hole. If there were sandbags to protect the hole from the rain Kenneth explained how he had extended the sandbag wall to protect his dog, too. That dog was his mate as much as any other soldier there.

Plans for his deployment out of Kandahar Airfield (KAF) in mid-April had been held back so the days waiting meant more time to write letters home. I loved getting the extra letters but I didn't like hearing Kenneth's frustration. *'That work I mentioned has been postponed for now so I'm still in KAF living the dream! ... How's life back in Newcastle?'* If the letters weren't very short, they were very long and full of detailed questions about his dog at home, 'K', and the welfare of Trevor his tortoise and how his dad was getting on with setting up the vivarium. I couldn't help smiling as I read his ramblings. Maybe there was a little bit of guilt in there for leaving us with his pets to care for (but we had always done that) or it was all about stringing out that connection – for as long as he could stay awake to write it all down. It was funny and lovely and I just wanted to reach out and give him a massive hug.

Getting a letter like that said one thing to me: he needed cheering up. He was going to miss his sister Stephanie's 21st birthday meal so I decided we would take a bluey and a pen with us and pass it around the table so every member of the family could add a message to Kenneth – as if he had been there with us. He loved it! In the best way we could we managed to get Kenneth at that table, and just imagining the food was enough for him. It was as if living on ration packs had caused him to hallucinate about his grandma's Chinese chicken curry, mince and dumplings and his favourite roast dinners. If I could have sent him a doggy bag I would have done it that night. Instead I wrote: 'We missed you, son,' knowing that he was missing us too.

Kenneth had just become a father too, to baby Hannah. He was so happy about the baby and desperate to see the little one, who was born just after he went on tour. It wasn't an easy situation with Kenneth so far away and I know Hannah was on his mind all the time. From the moment she was born she was in his letters. He was a father and he wanted to get home to see her, but he was also a dedicated dog soldier with a job to do.

For him, that April seemed to involve a lot of waiting and then waiting some more – for the 'push', as he described it. He told us the little he could about the scheduled briefings and particularly the training sessions which he loved and kept the dogs at the top of their game. Kenneth was pleased with Diesel and could see his potential, which was why he was eager to get the dog out on the ground. He was desperate to get the camera so he could send us photos of Diesel, his mate, going through his paces. I could sense his restlessness and the boredom in waiting for something to happen, but for us at home there was a greater distraction – the fear that something could happen to him.

From the time the conflict began in 2001 there was always enough on the TV to enable families back home to build a pretty clear picture of the hostility that faced our sons and daughters in Afghanistan. My son was out there, and that brought the war onto our doorstep, and in our own way we were living it, too, but it was no dream. And for Kenneth, home became much more than just where he lived.

Looking back it's amazing how quickly his being away became part of our daily lives. It was a good job that his sisters understood and were never jealous, because in a sense Kenneth was still with us – making us laugh, making us mad and making us run around him, all the while, unintentionally, being the centre of attention. Through his phone calls home and his letters, Kenneth, the cheeky chap, the joker in the Rowe pack, was as close to us as he could be for a dog soldier in Afghanistan.

He might not have been with me in person, and maybe he was too far away for me to 'read' (he always said I was a witch because I could always read his mind – he knew he could never hide anything from me), but his moods and concerns were right there in his blueys. The salutation was usually enough to set the mood – Hello Mam, Hi Parents, Olla Mamma, Howdy Mother – and hinted that he was upbeat and excited about something. I was always wary when I got a Hi Mam or just Hi. When that happened I prepared myself for a letter that was going to be along the lines of one of our late-night chats we had at home – the kind of conversation that started when no one else was around. We'd make a cup of tea and then he would tell me what was making him angry or sad, ask me for advice or just talk and reach conclusions himself. I would hold him and tell him it was all going to be OK and he must not worry.

We could still do that in a letter and my heart would pound when I read his sign-off: *'Cheers, Mam, you're a star as always. I couldn't survive without you by my side every step of the way. All my love as always. Ken xxx and Diesel xxx'*

We realised later that after he called and spoke to his dad on Thursday evening his plans to come home must have changed. I was still on my journey back from Carlisle when he called to tell Ken that he would be back at Bastion later. He must still have been at FOB Inkerman at that stage so it must have been after that that he asked to stay the extra day with the men of 2 Para. He found out that his replacement wasn't due out right away, which would have left the troops without a bomb dog and handler for 24 hours. Kenneth wouldn't have wanted that, so I understood why he volunteered to stay behind. And, knowing Kenneth as I do, I believe that he would have insisted he stayed.

He was killed just hours later.

I have a lot of 'blanks' from that time. I could blame the pills but the result is still the same – I feel ashamed. It's awful. I have gaps and I want to fill them but the memories are so fragmented: I start to remember and then I hit a blank. Then I feel I know something but then ... blank. I want it all back – the lost time. I often wonder, did I take too many pills to block out the pain?

Few people expected to be made welcome over the next couple of days and I'm sure that included visits from the military, but out of everyone we needed to see they were the people who could tell us what happened to Kenneth and what would happen next. I really needed to know.

The next day brought Major Chris Ham (now Lieutenant Colonel retired) and Staff Sergeant Iain Carnegie (now Captain Carnegie with the Australian Army) to the door. I'm sure we were everything they expected us to be, but we couldn't be anything else. Both knew Kenneth well and had served with him.

I wanted to hear that he was well liked and good at his job. I heard that Kenneth was all of that and more and that he would be sadly missed by everyone he had ever served with. And that he loved his family very, very much.

Iain and Chris were familiar names to me. Kenneth had talked about them since he joined the RAVC in 2005. Major Chris Ham had been his Commanding Officer at the Defence Animal Centre in Melton Mowbray and Iain his Company Quartermaster Sergeant (CQMS) in Northern Ireland, but they were in his world and now they were in our lounge, in full uniform, telling me how my son would be missed by everyone who had the pleasure of serving with him and who had spent time with him as their friend. They were talking about Kenneth. My son. I was in the room but in another way I was in another world. It was someone else's world. How could it be mine? I was listening to everything that was being said but it had no relevance to me.

As they left I heard them both offer their help to the family and ask Ken if he was all right. My husband, my gentle giant, said it all in a few words: 'I'm gutted but very, very proud of my son.'

When Ken came back into the room we sat together and cried.

I don't remember stopping.

It was good of Major Ham and Iain Carnegie to visit us at home. I realised later that they didn't have to make that drive from North Luffenham, 104 Military Working Dogs Support Unit and Kenneth's Army base, to Newcastle, but they wanted to. It was their personal choice and it couldn't have been easy for them either. Kenneth's death must have been as much of a shock to the other dog handlers and trainers as it was to us. They all seem to know each other, whether Army or RAF, and although we always think the military must take the news of a death in battle in their stride I now know that it's not like that at all. Kenneth was part of the Army's family as much as he was part of ours. They had lost one of their boys, one of their own.

Chapter 2

Man down!

'Thomo, you need to get down here now.' Captain Martyn Thompson (now Major Thompson) had just returned to his room after dinner and was ironing his kit for the next day when the call came in.

'What's up?' The Captain stepped into the Ops Room.

'It's Ken.'

'How bad?'

'I'm sorry, but all indications are we've lost him. The dog, too. We've planned for this, Thomo, so we all know what we need to do. We need to get our ducks in a row and do our best for him. Over to you.'

The ZAP number (initials and last three digits of the service number) that spilled out of the messenger in the Ops Room was Kenneth Rowe's: KR 366. It identified him as a casualty on the ground now on his way back to Bastion. Martyn Thompson saw it and knew what

35

had to be done. First he called Chris Ham. 'Chris, you can't repeat this but early reports are that we've lost one. It's the Geordie.' Rather Chris, who had been Kenneth's Commanding Officer in the UK, hear it from his friend than anyone else, and it would give him time to get himself together before the news came through officially just a short while later.

On the ground, the Army 'system' kicked in. Sergeant Major Frank Holmes had just finished his evening meal when he ran into a colleague heading for Bastion HQ. 'He's gone, Frank. The Geordie lad. He's gone.'

That's all the person said. Running in to find out more, Frank hoped the message had been mixed and there had been some confusion over the ZAP number, but sadly the information was confirmed. Frank had lost one of his best handlers and his best dogs. Not only had he lost one of the RAVC's rising stars as a handler and trainer, he had also lost a good soldier.

'I was devastated and I walked to the rest room where everyone had been ordered to go for the announcement, and with every step I found it impossible to hold back the emotion,' recalls Frank. The padre accompanied the Ops Commander who announced that the man down was Lance Corporal Kenneth Rowe of the RAVC and that his search dog, Sasha, had fallen with him.

'Some of the girls burst into tears and some of the men, too. Several of the guys left the room to punch the air outside, swear at God and smoke. The shock was part of it but more the fact that we all knew Ken Rowe. We had lived with him over the past four months at Bastion and shared work time and down time in his company. Some of us had known him longer than that. We had been with him, off and on, since his early days at the Defence Animals Centre (DAC) at Melton Mowbray and his first posting to Northern Ireland. The fact that someone had just told us that the handsome, cheeky Geordie lad was gone and his body was due in from the front line was totally unbelievable.

'I tried to believe it because the certainty of what had happened meant that we had a job to do and we were only going to do it well.'

A communications lock-down prevented the identity of the man down getting to the media and therefore the family before the Army could reach them in person. But there was still a fallen soldier on the ground.

Only twenty-four hours earlier Kenneth had called for a situation report. As part of the 2 Para battle group deployed from FOB Inkerman he was finally seeing the action he had been hoping for since he landed in Afghanistan on 18 March.

He had been assigned to a regiment that had seen and was still seeing some of fiercest engagements and the highest losses of the conflict so far. Every fighting unit over there wanted a dog and handler team alongside them; this was exactly what Kenneth was out there to do with his dog alongside him.

Never a lover of vehicle searches – although he would always do a stint on the gate – Kenneth was happier away from the patrol and search role at Kandahar Airfield and was soon firmly embedded with 2 Para at FOB Inkerman. The Paras took to his dog partner then, Diesel, too, and maybe too much as Kenneth often had to remind them that he was a working dog, not a playmate! A difficult call when home comforts are in such short supply.

Through April and May 2008 the dogs and handlers had to get used to moving around. The demand was constant and came from all bases: Kabul, Kandahar, Sangin, Inkerman, Kajaki, Musa Qala, Lashkar Ghar, Combat Logistic Patrols and Camp Bastion. It was a huge operation to manage, as R and R (Rest and Recuperation) was as important to factor into the mix as deployments if combat fatigue and the stress of being constantly posted from one situation to another were to be kept at bay.

While Kenneth had been at Kandahar and then FOB Inkerman, Sasha had been fighting her own war against the Taliban at Musa Qala. Lance Corporal Marianne

Hay had trained her well and with Sergeant Andy Dodds Sasha had become the RAVC's most capable search dog at the time. She was hot property, but no one would have grasped that from just looking at her.

Small, slight, fine-boned and pretty – that was Sasha. A lovely creamy-toned yellow Labrador with the sweetest nature but with high drive and nerves of steel. Dog soldier Marianne Hay had trained Sasha as a bomb dog in Northern Ireland. The pair had been the last Army dog team to leave the Province when the Army Dog Unit relocated to North Luffenham in 2007, but Marianne had used their time there to add a few skills to Sasha's CV. While the girl and dog team had successfully supported the police and the engineers there, Marianne had also worked hard on preparing Sasha for ops in Afghanistan. Sooner or later she knew her dog would need it.

It's an Army dog's life and a dog soldier's one to bear that the team that works together does not always stay together, and this was a hard truth for Marianne. She had formed a strong bond with Sasha but she had also prepared her well for theatre (action on the front line) and brought her on to the point where she could hit the ground running. And run she did.

Sasha was deployed to one of the most dangerous places in the world at the time; Musa Qala was known to be a hotbed of insurgent activity, and fighting was desperate and fierce. The Taliban considered the town to be their spiritual home and they wanted to take it back. Danger lurked on every corner, in every house, and on every street. Its labyrinth of underground tunnels that ran beneath the community hid a multitude of sins and sinister activities. It was the place where any arms and explosives search dog, even one of Sasha's calibre, was going to be challenged.

In no time at all Sasha was notching up 'find' after 'find'. It had been designated a 'high-activity' area and Sasha's skills were proving that classification was justified. Hidden weapons, mines, mortars, motors for rocket-propelled grenades, suicide vests … the list was endless. Sergeant Dodds felt safe working with Sasha, the dog who was earning herself a reputation: 'If it's hidden, Sasha will find it.'

Kenneth already knew Sasha was highly skilled. He had served with Marianne in Northern Ireland and the competitive friends had often verbally sparred over training techniques. Both were passionate about their dogs and there was mutual respect for each other's skills. It was what they were there to do but the work was intense and achieved in temperatures that could hit a relentless 40–50 degrees during the working day. The soldiers could look forward to going home on R and R, but the dogs were doing it all to be rewarded with a tennis ball, a meal and, if they were out in the desert, a good rest alongside their handler. The dogs were soldiers the same as the handlers – but the rewards were different. It was the ability to maintain the high drive to work and search without wavering in efficiency and success that put Sasha in a class of her own.

Sasha was holding her own against the heat and the workload. It was the height of summer – the period recognised as the 'fighting season' – with just 14 dogs to service regiments operating in seven locations. Everyone was under pressure. IEDs (Improvised Explosive Devices) were now the preferred weapon of the Taliban and just weeks earlier Ken and Diesel had been thrown from an Army Snatch Land Rover. Ken crawled out of the overturned vehicle covered in dust but unhurt; Diesel had injured his paw in the explosion and was taken back to Bastion for treatment and rest.

While Diesel recuperated, Reece became the dog in Ken's life, but it wasn't long before the dynamic duo were back on the front line protecting and saving life and limb.

Andy's new role was imminent and Kenneth was writing about going home but he was still waiting for confirmation of the date. Trouble was, with everything that was going on, the chances of it happening were looking increasingly slim. The intensity of the work was starting to show on Diesel and Ken had to report his concerns to his Sergeant Major, Frank Holmes. Diesel was seeking shade, and not just when he was on his downtime. He knew his dog was a tough cookie who had survived IEDs and being thrown from a Snatch, but if he was fading in the heat he would fail to detect. It was time for Diesel to take a rest.

And that was how Ken Rowe and Sasha came together. Ken needed a good reliable dog, and Andy was heading for a new role of Ops Sergeant, leaving Sasha up for grabs. Matching the right dog with the right handler in the right location wasn't Ken's decision but he put in a request for Sasha anyway. Frank Holmes felt it was a good match and Martyn Thompson headed out to FOB Inkerman to deliver Sasha to Ken. Moving the dog was considered easier than moving the man – all they needed was the change of dog for the intense weapons and search work ahead. It wasn't long before they were considered the best team in the area at the time, and Sasha continued to locate weapons, ammunition and IEDs, giving Ken plenty to call in to his commanding officer.

By the time Ken's July leave was confirmed, he and Sasha had been supporting 2 Para for over a month and the pair were very much part of the team. It had been a particularly hazardous operation from the start and it was taking its toll on the troops. The new threat, suicide bombers, had taken the lives of three of their men. Until then small-arms fire and the RPG had been the insurgents' weapons of choice but the arrival of the IED and the suicide bomber had made the fighting game more sinister and blurred the rules of engagement. It made the job of the dog and the soldier harder, too.

Ken was happy that Sasha was still providing consistent cover even during operations that could last ten to twelve hours in searing temperatures. She was just as enthusiastic as she had been on her first day, which meant Marianne Hay's training and the dog's own determination and intelligence were paying off. The bond that Sasha and Ken had formed in the relatively short time they had been paired was clear for all to see, and the men of 2 Para were relieved to have the dog and handler head their patrols.

Twenty-four hours before he was due to go on leave, Ken Rowe put a call in to Bastion for a situation report. The handler who was due to replace him was sick. This wasn't the news he was hoping for and it wasn't good news for 2 Para either. Ken didn't like the thought of the patrol going out without the support of a search dog. They were in bandit country and everyone was very much aware of the value of having a dog on the ground. He couldn't do it. He couldn't leave them. He lobbied his unit to allow him to stay until the changeover could take place. Then he could go on his R and R with some peace of mind.

His request to stay on was granted.

* * *

Throughout that fatal day the patrol had been shadowed by a group of insurgents. Sasha was already known to them; they were aware of the 'yellow dog' and her ability to locate their deadly weapons. She must have foiled hundreds of their plots and discovered tons of explosives and ammunition and it was no secret that having a bomb dog on duty reassured the troops.

The patrol was just three kilometres from FOB Inkerman when the enemy struck from three angles. As Ken and Sasha made for the roadside ditch, Sasha was blown off her feet – she had been targeted by RPG direct fire – and separated from Ken. Eyewitnesses reported that the brave dog rose out of the dust, shook herself down and ran towards her handler. Ken gathered her in to take cover with the others behind a low wall but a second RPG found them both. Man and dog fell together.

The exchange was fast and furious, with visibility restricted by the gun smoke, dust and debris kicked up by the enemy RPGs. In the kind of silence that creeps in when the battle subsides came the cry:

'Man down! Man down!'

The medic was already rushing to where Ken lay on the ground. A stretcher appeared alongside and the bearers lifted Ken swiftly and cleanly into it with Sasha's body at his side. It was a race against time to get them both to an area of safety before the team was spotted and picked off by an opportunist sniper.

Out of the chaos a Land Rover screeched to a halt. It was out of sight but just hearing the urgency of the engine was a comfort of a kind as the stretcher was hurried in its direction. 'Come on, lift! Let's go, go go!'

The Land Rover took off in a cloud of dust in the direction of FOB Inkerman, with everyone on board hoping they were still dealing with a casualty and nothing worse. The vehicle was jolting from side to side trying to cope with the scattered rocks which littered the dramatic rough terrain. Everyone was holding very tight onto their precious cargo.

Suddenly the vehicle lurched and Sasha slipped from the stretcher. The loud gasp from the back alerted the driver to a problem but it was too risky to stop and Ken had to remain their priority. It was clear he needed urgent medical attention. They already feared when they loaded her onto the stretcher that it was too late for poor Sasha.

The enemy was still out there and no doubt watching every move. They would have seen Sasha's limp and lifeless body lying stranded and out of reach. The men could not risk more casualties: they had no choice but to leave her.

Frank Holmes and Martyn Thompson waited at the hospital in Bastion for the helicopter bringing Ken in from Inkerman. They knew what they had to do when it arrived, but right at that moment, as Frank says, it was the constant stream of casualties that added to the fear and trepidation:

'The Paras had had another bad time of it and, from what I can remember, there seemed to be a whole lot of casualties pouring off the choppers. It must have been a hell of a day and I admit it was quite unnerving sitting there wondering what devastation we still had to go through.'

Frank heard another Chinook arrive and hoped it would be the one they were waiting for and for this part of the proceedings to be over.

Frank and Martyn went in to ID the body. They confirmed that it was Lance Corporal Kenneth Michael Rowe RAVC.

'As I looked at Ken lying there, I know it sounds odd, but a part of me was relieved that I could honestly tell his mother, when I called her in the next few hours, that he looked as if he was sleeping. As for the rest of it – I could not possibly explain.'

The Union Flag was lowered to half mast at Bastion. Sadly this was something that was happening more often during the summer of Op Herrick 8, but for the men and women of the RAVC's dog soldiers it was something they hoped they would never see for one of their own during the conflict. They hadn't lost a dog soldier since The Troubles in Northern Ireland.

'When a soldier is lost, the flag is flown at half mast and I could not believe that this time it was lowered for one of mine,' recalls Frank Holmes. 'I now hate flagpoles. What made it worse was the constant repeats on Sky News, and the added loss of Sasha extended the coverage and the agony for all watching. We thought of Ken's family, lovely people, who would be mourning their son. Believe me, the grief at Bastion and FOB Inkerman was palpable.'

Martyn Thompson was hearing major concern from the men and women in his command over the retrieval of Sasha. He was able to tell them that he had said, 'Bring the dog if you can,' but everyone was fully aware of the risks. The area was crawling with Taliban, making it impossible to return to the site without risking a life or limb. What Martyn and his colleagues didn't realise at the time was that the men of 2 Para had already made a silent promise to each other that they would reach Sasha – no matter what.

Moving in, under the noses of the Taliban, they lifted Sasha's body off the road and returned her to Inkerman. They said later that Ken's dog was regarded in the same way as her handler, as one of their own, and there was no way they were going to leave her alone or where she lay. It was a risky mission; the Paras were aware that the enemy would be watching and expecting the soldiers to return for their dog. For all they knew they could have been walking into an ambush or the body could have been booby-trapped. Undeterred by the obvious risks, the men brought Sasha in and handed her back to her family: the RAVC.

When Marianne and the others heard what the Paras had risked for Sasha, tears flowed: 'I had been tasked out to an Operation in FOB Gibraltar (FOB GIB), which was 10 to 15 km from where Ken was based at FOB Inkerman. It was known to be a risky area. I was with 3 Para and we were due to go on a task early in the morning. The plan was to leave really early in the morning before the light came up so we could move to positions before the enemy could see us.

'The helicopter dropped me at FOB GIB and got my admin squared away before we all tried to get some sleep. It was early but we also knew we had to be up early. No surprise that it took me forever to get to sleep. I remember just curling up on the sand with my helmet as a pillow and finally managing to drift off. Ironically, once it was dark someone woke me up and I was like, "Oh, for f***'s sake, it's time to go already?" But the guy just said, "Boss wants to see you." Straight away I knew someone had deffo been hurt.

'So I went. Quickly. "Look, a handler and his dog have been hit." My body became heavy and my mind raced … Who? What? They said they had little info but it was an RPG attack. I wanted to know who it was.

'They told me I could go through the sit rep/9 liner (situation report) that had been sent to see if could find a ZAP number. I was scrolling through the whole thing and the first listing that caught my eye was the last four numbers of Sasha's Service number. I was, like, no f***ing way has she been hit. Then I scrolled down more and more and there it was – confirmed. Then I saw Ken's ZAP number.

'At this point I was just skimming. I was sure they were just injured. Then I saw "KIA" in what seemed massive writing. I clocked it again. KIA – Killed in Action. I felt like I had had my guts ripped out completely. I felt so heavy and I really didn't want to believe it. The guys asked if I was OK and I was like, yeah, and went back to my rock to lie down.

'I lay there while everyone around me slept. The sky in Afghan is so clear that you wouldn't believe the amount of stars. Everything seemed silent but at night it was far from it. The noise of the Ops room is usually ongoing and the noise of the bugs and cricket things is like white noise – it's constant. I was there with around 150 guys but right then it felt like I was just sat in the middle of the desert with absolutely nothing and no one around me. I couldn't really think straight. I just sat with no thoughts, hearing no noise. Nothing.

'As I waited to be called to go on task I couldn't cry. By the time I was called to go on the op, between about 3 and 4am, I was so angry with myself because there was no space inside me to feel pain. I was angry Sasha had gone and I had let it happen and I was angry that I hadn't shed a tear for my colleague, Ken. My best friend used to always joke and say I had a heart of stone or that I was dead inside and in actual fact I started to believe it at this point.

'So I got asked if I was still up for going out. I was like, "Yes, of course." Off I went with my dog, Leanna, on a shit night patrol looking for a bunch of a***holes that had just done this to my mates. I was pretty pissed off by this point but knew I'd keep my head. Looking back, that patrol felt like the longest I had ever done but it was probably the shortest. I had been used to ops lasting weeks out on the ground and this was just 24 hours. The guys had a clear objective and it was due to be a quick in and out job.

'I can't remember exactly what we were there to do but we were supposed to get places in the dark without the enemy knowing, but about 5 minutes after leaving the FOB there was radio chat from the enemy – they had pretty much clocked us as soon as we had left. We were rather vulnerable as it was new territory to us.

'When we returned to the FOB I was told a Sea King hele was on its way for me. I told them I was fine and wanted to continue, but that didn't work. I was then told the hele was on its way and I would be 100 per cent on it – no discussion. I was so exhausted that I remember rolling into the belly of the big bird and just lying there while it took off. I got dragged into a space and left huddled by mailbags.

'I honestly can't remember what happened when I got back to Bastion. I am sure we would have been gathered many times but when they talked it was almost like I was under water and only hearing mumbling. It was difficult. I remembered Ken saying to me that he felt really lucky to have Sasha as his search dog as her performance was of such high quality. He was right, she was the best and I know he looked after her. I couldn't hug Sasha but I remember going to Leanna and begging a cuddle. I sat with her in her kennel for ages. Poor Leanna did her best to comfort me but I felt so guilty. I had lost Sasha and a good mate but I could not cry.

'I felt worse when I found out later that Sasha's body had not made it back with Ken's but then when I was told about the incredible bravery of the guys of 2 Para who had taken it upon themselves to go on a patrol the next morning to retrieve her it absolutely blew me away that they would consider her so highly that they risked their lives to bring her in. My gratitude to these guys remains endless.'

When Marianne heard that Sasha's body was due back into Camp Bastion she went to the hele pad to accept her.

'When I returned to the dog unit I lay her on the cold floor and unzipped her body bag. She lay there, not a mark on her body. She looked, as she always looked to me – perfect. Then I turned her over. There was blood and the wounds were deep, but there's no way you would think they would be enough to kill her. I guessed the shock would have been too much for her. I took a moment with Sasha and apologised a million times over before saying goodbye.'

The wheels of administration moved swiftly and with every eye on getting it right for the man, but there was also a large swell of feeling in getting it right for the dog, too. After all, they died as they served – together. If Kenneth Rowe was going home then it was the dog soldiers' wish that Sasha go home too and, more than that, she would join him on the flight back to RAF Lyneham. After a great deal of jumping through hoops and rewriting the rule book it was agreed that Ken and Sasha would be repatriated together.

Time was short. Due to the regulations and the heat, Sasha's body had to be cremated right away, and in the true tradition of the British Army the minds and skills of everyone pulled together to ensure that this canine hero returned in a fashion befitting her military status. There would be no flag-draped coffin for her, so the armourers pitched in with a 5-inch diameter shell casing, engraved with her name and dates, to hold her ashes. It was finished with a polished-wood stopper and the whole thing gleamed to the point that it made anyone who looked at it blink. It was a fine tribute to a fine dog.

Martyn Thompson and Frank Holmes were in charge of the arrangements for the repatriation of Ken Rowe and Sasha back to the UK, and for Frank the ordeal was nothing short of surreal: 'Never did I think I would need the repatriation training I received on my drill instructor's course. To be honest, at that time it was treated with a touch of "gallows humour" at Pirbright (the Army training centre) – one of the guys dressed up as the mum or girlfriend, the chaplain is present and we practised for what seemed like a week for something you think you are never going to do for real. I never thought I would do it in my own unit. But there we were, with just two days to get it right for Ken and now Sasha, too. It was bloody heart-breaking.'

Ken and Sasha would not be returning alone. Corporal Jason Barnes, of the Royal Electrical and Mechanical Engineers (REME), had been killed two days before Ken and would be on the same flight. The Paras had been practising the repatriation drill although they were, sadly, used to the format now. Afraid that they would look amateurish beside the Para bearers, Frank spoke to their Sergeant Major and it was agreed that the bearer parties would approach the C17 in line rather than the usual side-by-side.

Selecting the bearers was no easy task. The honour of carrying a fallen colleague has its mix of practical (for height) and emotional (who could hold it together long enough). Everyone volunteered for the job but only six could be selected – amongst them was Sasha's previous handler, Andy Dodds, and, to steady the coffin at the rear, Frank Holmes. Army Chaplain Paul Gallucci knew the unit well – and he knew Ken, too. He had served with them all in Northern Ireland and was well aware of the value of the dog soldiers in theatre and the deep bond that exists between the dog unit and the infantry on the ground. To complete the proper send-off, Marianne Hay was chosen to carry Sasha's ashes onto the plane. It was the last thing she could do for the dog she loved, trained and served alongside.

Camp Bastion: 11pm, Sunday 27 July

Someone from the REME produced a hip flask. It was a welcome start to the proceedings and broke a little ice. Gazing into the darkness it looked like a disappointing turnout at first, despite there being two men making the return home. The cavernous hold of the C17 gaped open, its ramp down ready to accept the two flag-strewn coffins that sat in the back of the waiting field ambulances. As the lights came up to illuminate the runway the beams caught the truth of the scene. Row upon row of uniformed personnel were waiting in silence. It seemed as if the whole of Camp Bastion had turned out.

Certainly Frank's wish to get as many dog soldiers there as possible had been granted and the Engineers at the Joint Forces EOD (Explosives Ordnance Disposal) had performed miracles. They had worked with Ken and Sasha and were used to the job split: the dog soldiers locate the explosives and the bomb squad blow them up. It was a good relationship and they felt the loss as keenly as Frank and the rest of his team. Using all their powers and man-management skills, the EOD had successfully brought in all but three of their teams from the various FOBs to attend the ceremony. These were the faces, many tear-stained, shining out of the darkness.

The bearers took the strain of the weight of the coffin first in their hands and then on their shoulders. The practice weight was lighter than this but the responsibility was heavier. Frank Holmes took the rear position, ready to instruct and push up as the party took the slow and careful incline up the ramp and into the body of the plane. Sasha's former handler, Sergeant Andy Dodds, took front left position: 'The concentration was immense. The plane is meant to take cargo so the ramp is designed to be smooth underfoot and as I looked ahead to prepare for my first step up I couldn't help noticing the number of people present and the dogs, too. As I took that first step onto the ramp I became very aware of my legs and feet. I only wanted them to do what my head was telling them. I'm sure all of us were feeling the same. Marianne was walking alone behind us, her arms around the shell casing containing Sasha's ashes. I've no doubt she was trying her very best to hold back tears right to the point where she placed the casing at the head of the coffin.

When Marianne Hay accepted the honour of carrying Sasha's ashes onto the plane at Camp Bastion she did it to ensure that the dog she trained was repatriated in the way of a hero, to sit at the feet of another hero, her friend and fellow search dog handler, Lance Corporal Kenneth Rowe. With tears welling in her eyes for the loss of the dog she considered closest to her heart and the man she considered to be one of the most talented handlers in the team, Marianne held the brass casing close to her body. As she walked through the soft sound of stifled sobbing, passing colleagues lining the route, she managed to keep her head.

Step by slow step she followed the bearer party up the steep ramp and into the darkness of the body of the plane. It was hard. Hard to do and hard to let go. After setting down the coffin the party paused a moment and hugged each other.

Sergeant Dodds added: 'Getting through the formalities just as we planned and setting Ken down on the plane was the easier bit. It was saying our personal last goodbyes, the prayers and the group hug that gave most of us the licence to let go of our feelings. The darkness robbed us of a view of the giant C17 lurching into the sky above Bastion but we could hear it loud and clear and knew that it would dip its wings for the final farewell – that was the hardest part. Then, for Ken and for all of us, we had to get the teams back on the ground and take the fight right back to the Taliban.'

Chapter 3

For Queen and country – The Troubles

Ken's death in July 2008 had highlighted the growing need and respect for the dog soldiers within the wider Army. The demand for search dogs in Afghanistan had massively increased. The patrols appreciated the reassurance of having a search dog with them making safe their route ahead, so the pressure weighed heavy on the RAVC and specifically the men and women of 104 MWD unit to supply the demand. As a Combined Forces operation the pressure radiated out to the Danish and the Americans to provide additional search dog cover too. But the Brit dogs, from the Army and the RAF, were working hard to rise to the challenge. Trouble was, they couldn't get enough of them on the ground.

Ken Rowe had volunteered to stay on and pick up his R and R later because his replacement had fallen ill and would be out later than expected to support 2 Para. He had been working closely with the unit and was well embedded with them at FOB Inkerman, which was a small but highly volatile spot. Ken was their dog soldier and Sasha was their dog. They already knew that Ken was thorough, trustworthy and a cheeky Geordie and they knew Sasha was a lean, keen and effective search dog. Their relationship had been forged while they lived in sun- and rain-blasted holes in the sand and waited and waited for the attention of the enemy that they knew would show itself – they just didn't know when. Sasha's ability to locate deadly devices and hidden weapons and arms had been a literal lifesaver. There was no way Ken was going to leave the men vulnerable. He was staying – and so was Sasha.

Operation Herrick 8 was proving the toughest yet. Death and serious injury were daily occurrences and the regular procession of hearses carrying flag-draped coffins through Wootton Bassett was educating the public in the extent of the sacrifice. The media coverage was also responsible for delivering the emotions attached to the loss into everyone's home in a very visual way. Even for families untouched by a death or disfigurement, the impression of what was actually happening in Afghanistan was real and almost tangible.

For many of the senior members of the RAVC dog unit this was a reminder of the past and, at some level, the continuing threat in Northern Ireland. Many of the Commanding Officers in Afghanistan had served during The Troubles and others, like Ken Rowe, had later cut their teeth in the Province.

The Army Dog Unit, Northern Ireland, was formed on 1 May 1973. From its base in Ballykelly, County Londonderry, the unit provided critical support to the British Army who first posted troops to the Province in 1969. Only expecting to be needed for a few weeks to support the Royal Ulster Constabulary (RUC), the Army quickly realised that it would take more than short-term peacekeeping activity to quell the violent and ongoing clashes that had broken out between the Protestants and Catholics. By July 1973 the Army Dog Unit found itself at the heart of The Troubles when it lost the first of four of its number to terrorist activities.

Corporal Bryan Criddle, BEM, was the first of their fallen. He was patrolling the border at Clogher in County Tyrone with C Squadron, The Royal Tank Regiment, when his search dog, Jason, indicated (pointed out explosives) on a milk churn, one of several set out in a horseshoe formation. Bryan was working in recognised 'bandit country': if his dog was telling him explosives were present – they were. What he could not know was that the terrorists were watching. The milk-churn bomb was detonated remotely, leaving Bryan with life-threatening head injuries. He was helicoptered out to Musgrave Park hospital but lost his battle for life four days later. Jason was blown 30 feet in the air but by some miracle survived. Colleagues reported that the dog went into protective mode the second Bryan went down and had to be pulled off his master as he wouldn't let anyone get close to help. Jason was airlifted, too, and after a veterinary check-over was transferred to the kennels at the Maze Prison to recuperate.

Corporal Criddle was killed just weeks after being awarded the British Empire Medal (BEM) for his service with the Army Dog Unit in Northern Ireland; in July Jason had been awarded his 'wings' for completing 1,000 flying hours in helicopters operating between the garrison and the border to carry out his duties. This was recognition for the soldier and the dog, but it also drew attention to the unique role of the entire unit.

At that time the Army Dog Unit was a relatively small part of the RAVC, but its special skills were making a difference in Northern Ireland where the terrorist threat was often not just hidden from human eyes but it shifted in shape and composition all the time. In addition to the RAVC, dog handlers were recruited from volunteer dog soldiers within all regiments and corps of the Army and the dogs were trained in three disciplines: guard/attack dogs (known as Snappers or Land Sharks), tracker dogs (known as Groundhogs), and vehicle search dogs and arms and explosives search dogs – the Wagtails. The dogs and the soldiers were lifesavers no matter which of three disciplines they excelled in, but they were also targets.

In 1974 the then Commander Land Forces Northern Ireland, Major General Peter Leng, MC MBE, granted the ADU NI RAVC the right to wear a Red Paw badge in their berets to the left of their regimental cap badge. The enamel badge, measuring a quarter of an inch, was to unite the members of this specialist unit. The Red Paw badge represented the bloody paws of the dogs who carried out their duties, often walking on broken glass and in the shadow of death. The dog soldiers wore it with pride.

On the Bank Holiday weekend, 25 May 1991, Corporal Terry 'Geordie' O'Neill and his colleague Corporal Darren Swift, 'Swifty', were with their dogs, Blue and Troy, in the exercise yard at the Army barracks at North Howard Street Mill when a terrorist hurled a 'coffee-jar' bomb (containing Semtex, a detonator and 'shipyard confetti' – nuts, bolts, nails, rivets, etc) from the fire escape of the snooker hall next door. The homemade bomb landed at the soldiers' feet, killing Geordie instantly and taking Darren Swift's legs – and a finger – clean away. Blue and Troy miraculously survived the blast but needed veterinary care for their burnt paws. One life was taken and the other changed forever in one brief, brutal and deliberate act of violence.

Terry O'Neill was the last dog soldier to die in Northern Ireland but in the campaign that became known as Operation Banner (1969–2007) 763 military personnel lost their lives. After a deployment that spanned 38 years, the British Army left the Province. The dog handlers felt a definite wind-down as Op Banner drew to an end and their relocation as 104 MWD to North Luffenham became a reality.

At midnight on 31 July 2007 the Army Dog Unit Northern Ireland ceased to exist. The closing parade at Ballykelly marked the end of an era; a bitter-sweet period of living in a community riddled with fear while enjoying unrivalled camaraderie. It was where the Red Paw badge became a mark of distinction and symbol of courage. Young soldier Ken Rowe wore his with pride.

By 10 August 2007 North Luffenham was home to 104 Military Working Dog Support Unit and Ken was part of the 'lumping and dumping' of equipment at the St George's Barracks. For the next five months he played a key role in establishing the new unit out of everything that had made its way out of Northern Ireland and, at the same time, continuing to improve his skills and knowledge as a dog handler. Northern Ireland had been his first posting and it had given Ken a platform to showcase his skills and get himself known. He quickly gained a reputation for having a thirst for knowledge and a desire to progress his dog, himself and his career. He was also known for his level of fitness and skill as a footballer.

Encouraging everyone in the unit to take part in a four-mile run, three or four times a week – with the dogs – was not everyone's idea of fun, but to Ken Rowe is was a great way to beat the boredom of the wind-down. According to Frank Holmes, who assessed Ken out there as part of the veterinary services training evaluation team, he was '… quite simply a dream to manage. He was fit and friendly, except when he had a beer. Then he was a pain! He was keen to work and volunteer and, most importantly, he always had a smile on his face.'

When it came to dogs Ken Rowe was in his element. His Northern Ireland tour gave him the chance to handle a series of Protection Dogs, known in the Army as Land Sharks – all hair, teeth and attitude on the end of a leash. German Shepherd Max and Black Labradors Odie and Jackdaw proved challenging, but that's what Ken loved the most. He had a way with dogs that others couldn't handle, and that's one of the reasons why he stood out from the crowd. There were always the dogs that didn't live up to their potential because, like people, they are individuals who may have all the credentials on paper but lack the ability to apply those skills in practice. Ken could sort the wheat from the chaff and knew when a dog didn't have what it took to work well in that environment. It was Odie that Ken took to the most, so much so, in fact, that he brought him back to Newcastle. The dog was looking for a good home for retirement so Ken came up with a fail-safe plan to give this dog a richly deserved, peaceful home for the rest of his life. Odie went to live on a farm in Bedlington, far away from his life in the Army.

It was while Ken was in Northern Ireland that he had his first encounter with losing a colleague; worse still, it was Ken who discovered the body. It was Christmas at RAF Aldergrove and while the other protection dog handlers were making the best of a bad lot away from home, one young soldier, Lance Corporal John Murphy, decided that, for some reason, enough was enough. Ken was concerned because when he had last seen John he thought he looked very down and preoccupied. Christmas was not a time to be anything but happy and in party mood; that's what Ken was used to. It was probably the thought of someone not enjoying themselves that drove Ken to find his friend and cheer him up.

What he found when he reached John's quarters was to stay with Ken in his waking and sleeping hours. He found his friend had taken his own life, and despite Ken's desperate attempts to revive him it was too late. Finding a friend and colleague, a young man like himself but with a family, was hard on Ken and he looked to the more experienced members of the unit for advice. Frank Holmes was well placed to keep a close eye on him and to make sure the cheeky Geordie in Ken Rowe was never too far away. One thing Frank knew for sure was that Ken's family would support him through the trauma and get him back on track for what lay ahead.

As for John's widow, Rachel, and their two children – Steven, aged three, and Emily, aged two when he died – life changed from that moment. She remembers Kenneth Rowe very well, not just as John's friend and colleague but for how he helped her to cope when her world stopped turning. 'Ken was a huge comfort to me and the children after John's death, and he took time out of his leave to help me with administrative tasks. I want to tell you about one incident that occurred after John's death which will reiterate what a kind, generous man Ken was, putting his own feelings aside to help others.

'Shortly after we lost John, in order to assist me with admin that needed sorting, the Army offered me a designated driver so I didn't have to drive around Northern Ireland by myself. Ken offered to do this out of his leave allowance and I was so pleased that it was someone I knew.

'One afternoon we went to pick up Steven from pre-school – Ken waited at the door. Steven came out of the building and looked at Ken and said, "Daddy?" quizzically as he had often seen his daddy and Ken together. Fighting back tears, Ken lifted him up and gently placed him in his car seat saying, "I'm not your daddy; I'm your Uncle Ken." Poor Ken was really upset and I know he was fighting a huge personal battle by being there for me and the children. But that was the kind of man he was. And I will never forget that, and neither will my children.'

Chapter 4

The dogs of war – deployment to Afghanistan

It is felt by some that the death of Major Alexis Roberts of 1st Battalion the Royal Gurkha Rifles in October 2007 altered the corps' direction and changed it forever. Major Roberts was killed instantly when the Vector vehicle he was travelling in at the head of a 30-vehicle convoy took the full force of an IED. The convoy was on the road between Camp Bastion and Kandahar Airfield, which had already gained the nickname 'IED alley'. At the inquest it was revealed that the home-made bomb – a cooking pot tightly packed with explosives – was triggered remotely by the watching Taliban using a 300-metre command wire. A series of delays, including vehicle breakdowns, resulted in the air support having to withdraw due to lack of fuel. As the convoy travelled the last 19 miles to Kandahar without air cover it fell prey to the roadside bomb.

With IEDs proving a greater and more frequent risk than ambush, small-arms fire and RPG attacks in Afghanistan, the focus fell on the RAVC to provide more search dogs to go in to detect the new threat. Taking the model that had been developed in Northern Ireland, the dog soldiers were deployed.

OPERATION HERRICK 8

In March 2008, in order to service the demand for dogs in two theatres of conflict, Iraq and Afghanistan, the Army had no choice but to split the unit, sending half the stock of fully operational dogs to each location. For Ken Rowe this meant deployment to Afghanistan. Having only five days rather than the expected two weeks for the handover, they had only a relatively short time to acclimatise to the blistering heat and get the dogs used to working in the desert environment. There were always a host of new smells to compute and a different terrain to work in. It was far from the green grass and black earth of home; this was a whole new ball game for many of the dogs – and it was a ball game, every time. For the reward of a tennis ball the search dogs looked for hidden weapons, ammunition and explosives. And in Afghanistan, as it was in Northern Ireland, the terrorists were always upping the threat.

It soon became clear that the Taliban were becoming more ruthless and their weapons more sophisticated. Devices such as the pressure plate had a low metal content, making detection more difficult, and the new and deadly IED was proving too efficient as a roadside bomb. The search dogs needed to increase their capabilities, this time specific to Afghanistan. These were new threats and the skills to locate them needed to be added to the dogs' knowledge bank. The dog soldiers were now recognised by the wider Army as a principal asset in the fight against the Taliban.

Ken Rowe was one of the chosen few to go forward for special search dog handling duties. His time in Northern Ireland had stood him in good stead. As a protection dog handler he had worked all over the Province, where there remained the possibility of a hidden threat and an underlying level of terror activity. He had lived with that knowledge and worked dogs in that environment, which made him an obvious candidate for the work in Afghanistan. He also got on with everyone, and that was important, too, as out on the ground everyone would be living cheek by jowl and whisker – with the dogs.

Frank Holmes and Martyn Thompson had created the team to carry out the task. The increased team of 14 search dogs (as opposed to nine on the previous tour) included broad skills, experience and high drive: the handlers offered the same qualities. Eleven search dog handlers – six men, five women – who could also cover on vehicle search and protection if need be (although there were additional handlers and dogs along to specifically carry out those duties) made up the 'human' side of the partnerships. The canine team included three substitute dogs – Battle Casualty Replacement (BCR) dogs – in case others got tired or sick. Even if Frank had thought they might need to replace a dog, he never thought they would lose a soldier.

Martyn Thompson was happy with the team: 'We had a good bunch of people, skilled handlers and soldiers, so we knew that we could offer a high competence level to support the infantry out there. We knew we had the right dogs and the right people to team up to cover what was needed in each of the identified "hot spots" and FOBs. In Ken Rowe I also had someone who could make even this kind of challenge go smoothly. I had my "go-to guy". If I asked Ken to go and do something, I knew it would be done. But I soon learnt not to ask too many questions about how he did it!

'One of the first concerns we had for the dogs out there was heat stress. If the dogs were suffering heat stress their natural instinct to seek shade would, sooner or later, overcome their high drive to search. The result would, potentially, be disastrous for all concerned. I shared his concern with the team, and Marianne Hay suggested that the use and the timing of the air-con at the kennels at Bastion could, potentially, have a detrimental effect on the dogs naturally acclimatising to the heat. It seemed a better idea to switch the air-con off and build a pool. But how do you build a swimming pool in the desert?

'It seemed I had planted a seed in Ken's mind. When he asked me to come and have a look at his doggy plunge pool I could hardly believe my eyes. I wanted to ask where on earth he had managed to pilfer what looked like a tent lining to hold the water, never mind the metal struts and the pallets that formed the sides. It transpired that the waterproof lining had been "borrowed" from our American cousins on the base and the rest had been sought out and gathered up from various places where they happened to be lying around. When I asked Ken "How? Where? And what?" I got the simple answer: "You don't need to know, boss. It's in the kennels so no one's going to see it!"

'What I also never found out was how he managed to strike a deal with a local contractor to empty and refill the pool on a weekly rota! What I do know is that Ken's pool was no doubt a lifesaver and it gave the dogs and the handlers a chance to blow off steam. It also gave the handlers some valuable bonding time with the dogs away from the heat and the dust of the day. It was pretty austere out there and it was easy to go feral after a while – well, the guys, not the girls. Bushy hair and beards were inevitable, especially as there wasn't a wife or girlfriend to smarten up for. When they were doing their job they were "on it" and when it was down time they made the best of it.

'Ken's pool was a godsend, and over the following weeks it was adapted and improved. If only the

Americans had known how grateful the Brits were for their generous waterproof donation! But that was Ken Rowe all over. When I went to see him at FOB Inkerman he had pretty much turned into "Bob the Builder"! He had commandeered an abandoned Afghan mud hut and turned it into a first-class dog kennel. I popped my head inside and found the dogs languishing in the shade, happy and healthy. It would be warm at night, too, so, looking around, the dogs had the best of the accommodation for sure. There were no power sockets so entertainment was pretty basic, but the good old pack of cards came in handy and Monopoly marathons to fill the waiting hours that can be the downside of the job: the hours waiting for something to happen and then fearing that it will. But after seeing that I realised I didn't need to worry about Ken coping out there; he was doing just fine. I truly believed that if we gave Ken a cave, a twig and a supply of baler twine and came back in a week he would show us a palace.

'Ken Rowe was one of those lads who could just make things happen, not for himself but to benefit everyone else around him. Wherever he was, Inkerman or Kandahar, he was quickly known as the good-looking guy with the dog!'

Identity became important, especially at Camp Bastion where every unit and regiment was represented, usually by flying their flag. Frank Holmes didn't want his unit to be overlooked, so, after having some flags made he was on the lookout for a flagpole or two.

'We were located right next to Bastion HQ and the Detention Centre so we were fairly central, and as everyone else had a flag I decided we weren't going to be left out.

'After about a week of trying to tap up the REME welders, with no luck, I was getting pretty frustrated. It was at about this time I found Ken Rowe and his mate Sean Cheatham hanging around in the rest room late one night. It was around 10pm and there was no need for them to be there so I had to ask them what they were up to. The response I got was: "Don't ask!"

'The next day a cracking flagpole had appeared at the side of the office. It was covered in a tarpaulin – but not for long. I got the lads to repaint it, plant it, and it stayed there until the day we left! It turned out that Ken and Sean had conducted their own special ops tour of Bastion in search of a suitable flagpole. Allegedly the Estonians had one to spare … or so the story went. I still think we would have been on the brink of another Cold War if their scouting party had been successful in tracking it down. Apparently they were fuming!'

Sport matters, even in the desert. When you think it's too hot to walk it's never too hot to play football or undertake the Bastion 5k race series. When Ken wasn't driving everyone mad with his Geordie 'Toons' CD he was out taking part in or organising some kind of activity to give everyone a break from the job. Whatever they decided to do was almost always for charities such as Help for Heroes, which was still in its infancy then. One of the more unusual events is 'Beat the Dog' – which is an Army favourite. It's a staged version of man versus dog. Always ready for action, the protection dogs are set to run after the brave contestants, all watched by a betting audience baying for a chance to see their officers flattened by the dogs. All in a good cause, the fun and games on that tour raised over £10,000, and Ken played a big part in it all. His gregarious character and charm as participant and organiser were a winner every time. He just drew people in.

According to his mates, if there was one thing that Ken Rowe enjoyed as much as his family, his job and a Sunday roast it was having a good moan. But the moaning only came in bursts and it was quickly over, as he often said in his letters home: 'Oh well, I feel better getting that off my chest!' If there was one thing that really got on his nerves and that of every search dog handler it was being assigned vehicle searches. In his mind if he was searching vehicles then he was not doing the job he had been trained to do and so it followed that if he wasn't with his dog searching ahead of an infantry unit on the ground the men could be at risk. What Frank Holmes wanted him to understand, and he knew that Ken did understand really, was that it had to be that way for the health and safety of the handler and the dog.

'I know it frustrated the hell out of our lads and lassies. They just wanted to be getting on with the job they had trained to do, and believe me it was difficult to ignore what they were telling me, but I had to. Pulling away from the intensity and highly stressful search dog work was not intended to frustrate anyone but to benefit everyone.

'I was well aware that we had lost handlers on previous tours due to the stress of the job and I had already decided we weren't doing that again. Certainly not on my watch. But we had one major problem, even though we had more dogs and handlers than ever before: we still didn't have enough for everyone who wanted them.

'My initial plan was to rotate the handlers every month to avoid the infantry units thinking they owned the dog working with them. Instead I "surged" the dogs to the terrorist hotspots and then back to Bastion. The handlers preferred this approach, and it was easier to move the right dog to the right place rather than always move the person. It also meant we could service the special operations and progress new initiatives to keep us two steps ahead of the Taliban rather than a dangerous two steps behind.'

Each of the hotspots had its own particular identity and threat level which could change overnight, depend-

ing on where the enemy felt more confident of 'success'
or were best placed to try out a new explosive device
on the troops. Several of the locations including Sangin,
Kajaki and Kabul were kept as standing tasks and
always had dogs and handlers, while the Combat
Logistic Patrols, including FOBs Inkerman and
Gibraltar, were surged from Bastion. At the time, this
provided a more fluid and effective approach to a
conflict offering ever-increasing challenges, and Ken
and Diesel often found themselves in the thick of the
action.

Ken was concerned about Diesel. When they were
both thrown from the Snatch Land Rover in an IED
strike Ken emerged shortly after, a little shocked but
covered in sand and laughing with his mates. Diesel
suffered an injury to his paw and had to be withdrawn
from duty. Ken teamed with Reece for a while but
when Diesel returned and started to show signs of heat
stress Ken knew he needed to retire his dog – and that
is when Sasha came into his life.

Chapter 5

Sasha enters the theatre

Sasha's story was similar to Ken's: she too gained all her Ops skills in Northern Ireland and from very early on showed all the signs of becoming something very special. Unusually, Sasha was procured in Belfast. The normal route was to recruit dogs at the DAC and train them there, but Lance Corporal Marianne Hay was about to start her search dog course in Northern Ireland before going on Operations in the Province so Sasha became her trainee.

'Sasha was a very clever dog and a very challenging character at first but somehow I knew she would reward my patience if I just stuck with her. Everything a good search dog needed was there in her: she was intelligent, inquisitive and obedient and she clearly had a high drive for the job. She wanted to search and she wanted that tennis ball at the end of it!

'I hoped my Army experience would add to our partnership and help bring her on. I had already completed a tour of duty in Iraq and worked search dogs with the British and American special operations engineers. I was pretty pleased with that but I don't think Sasha could have been too impressed because it still took me about four months to fully gain her trust and start to really bond with her. But once that initial part was over, we made quite a team.

'Sasha excelled at everything that was asked of her. We had an incredible three years together as a search dog team in Northern Ireland, and we covered all operations with the police, engineers and covert operations. I was kept busy as acting chief trainer and licensing the protection dogs to be used by the Northern Ireland security guard service after we left.

'To be honest, Sasha was not just a search dog, she was an all-rounder. Her agility skills were second to none and she always turned heads when I showcased her skills at all the usual dog and handler demonstration events. Even the RAF handlers were impressed. I'm sure they didn't expect such a relatively small, fine-boned and delicate creamy-coloured little Lab to scale a nine-foot wall, negotiate the parallel bars and jump through hoops of fire as if she was taking a walk in the park. She was awesome to watch!

'I liked that about Sasha – she was always surprising people. She was a very pretty dog, not butch in any way. She had a small, slim face and kind eyes. And her body was trim and toned. If she had been born human I think she would have been a catwalk model by day and fearless action hero Lara Croft by night. She could be every inch the loving and devoted Andrex puppy pet in her down time, but when the Army asked her to show the other side of her character she displayed the grit and determination of a war dog.

'Sasha lapped up all the training that I offered her. I'm sure I even got her to walk backwards for me! She could have outmanoeuvred Pudsey the dancing dog on *Britain's Got Talent* any day. Our time together in Northern Ireland provided the perfect opportunity to prepare her for Ops in Afghan. I did a lot of work with her to discover her threshold and focusing on buried explosives. I made it fun for her, but there was little fun ahead. I wanted Sasha to be my dog out there not just because she was the best but because by that time she had become my best friend, too. When I lost a friend and colleague to suicide that year (2007) I felt very alone, especially as my accommodation was set away from everyone else. That was the downside of being female in what had previously been a man's world. It was Sasha who helped me through all of that. She was my rock and always there for me in the special way that only dogs can be … just there for us without having to be anything but themselves. That special time together strengthened our bond for sure and made us the best of friends.'

Operation Herrick 8 loomed large and Marianne knew what would happen next. She knew that when the selectors saw what a good little working dog Sasha had become her dog would be on a plane out to Afghanistan.

'The Army wanted and needed their best dogs in Afghanistan, and Sasha was, without doubt, one of the best dogs we had at the time. I just hoped that I would be the handler going with her.

'Shortly after my colleague died I was called back to the UK for pre-deployment training. It soon became obvious that travelling from Belfast by plane with Sasha was only going to cause logistical problems so I had to stay on the mainland and was assigned another dog for the training ops. I had reclassified Leanna, a lovely and very springy springer spaniel just a few months earlier so I knew she was a good dog and there was little doubt that we would get through the training fine together.

'We completed the course and put in a great deal of good search work with the Royal Engineers, so it was no great surprise when I was told that I would be re-teamed with her for Afghanistan. At first I didn't really mind because Sasha wasn't going to be deployed so I just assumed that she would be waiting for me at North Luffenham when I got back from the tour. Sadly, for both of us, the situation changed overnight. It happened, just as I thought it would, Sasha was down for the tour after all and would be going out as a Battle Casualty Reserve (BCR) – but not with me.

'I shed more than a few tears over that decision. It wasn't easy to say goodbye to my best friend so we had plenty of hugs and I told her things I knew she wouldn't tell another living soul. I don't think I could have said more, even if I have known that would be our last goodbye.'

Sasha and the 13 other search dogs were flown into Kandahar and then transferred, with the handlers and all their gear and equipment, by Hercules C130 to Camp Bastion. They only had a few days to acclimatise to the heat and the terrain and carry out a formal handover with the outgoing team. There was no 'down time' – the Taliban didn't take days off and they didn't have any respect for the Army's needs. The bullets and the bloodshed continued 24/7, and as soon as Sasha put a paw on the sand she started to prove herself an asset to the team. For the first two months she worked on the ground doing what she had been trained to do. Marianne had taught her little creamy Lab well and she was becoming a literal lifesaver.

Through March and April Sasha had been settling into her new role and the ways of a new handler. Matched with Andy Dodds she headed for Musa Qala, where danger lurked on every corner. Marianne was still hopeful that Sasha would come her way while they were out there, and even though Leanna was working really well she couldn't help thinking and worrying about Sasha.

Sasha had been searching and finding on a regular basis and made a name for herself as a 'must-have' dog. Musa Qala and Sangin were proving to be two of the deadliest hotspots in Helmand. Andy was on the run-up to being transferred to a new role, but the pressure was full-on to keep stacking up the finds. It had already been a hard tour, and now it had every prospect of getting harder. Confident that Sasha was a good dog with a high drive meant he was in safe paws.

Sasha seemed to have a gift for finding anything and everything the Taliban left in her path, which meant Andy always had the great pleasure of seeing the long list of 'finds'. Marianne, as Sasha's trainer, was still hoping that she would be in a position to handle the dog in Afghan but it just wasn't happening. She was so close to Sasha but it might as well have been a million miles away, too.

Ken and Diesel were firmly embedded with 2 Para in the Upper Sangin Valley where the cheeky Geordie needed all of his sense of humour to offset the pressure of being constantly watched by the Taliban. Never a moment of true rest, always a half-sleep snatched when possible. Early in the tour, when they were attached to the Surge Battalion (3 Para), the pair were hitting trouble spot after trouble spot. But Ken, being Ken, could always find the funny side in spending days dug into a sand hole in the rain, or sheltered from a sandstorm – with a dog – praying for snow or just any other weather for a change. And there were the times he reached out from the darkness of that hole carved out of the sand, picked up a pen and some paper and wrote to his mother at home in Newcastle.

Chapter 6

Home – RAF Lyneham

Iain Carnegie had been given the responsibility of handling the bearer party at RAF Lyneham and he remembers waking early on the morning of Ken's repatriation and feeling nervous.

'I was fully aware of the responsibility but it hit me doubly that morning. We had to do the best we could for our mate and his family, who I knew would still be in pain. I had met Lyn and Ken senior at the pre-deployment send-off. It's not often that you get to meet a soldier's parents, but once I had I could understand why Ken was so proud of them and his roots. The next time I saw them was the day after they had been told their son had been killed. That experience will stay with me forever. Now Ken was coming home to his family and everything needed to be and had to be spot on.

'Having been involved with several military funerals I knew that if there was one thing that was common to all it was how the reality of the situation could suddenly

85

hit home with the bearer party. I knew every individual that would be carrying Ken and so I knew it would help to keep everything deliberate and functional with no room to manoeuvre or think beyond what we were doing until it was over.

'As the C17 came into view the pilot dipped the wings as a sign of respect and the huge grey hulk came in to land. Thankfully there is a procedure to follow; that was one big help to me and I knew it would help the six guys that I had set marching towards the ramp of the aircraft. I remember the eerie stillness and the low "tick, tick, tick" of the engines cooling.

'With practised precision the lads placed Ken on their shoulders and, not because I sensed anyone's unease but because I wanted to, I went to each man in turn and gave them a pat on the shoulder and asked if they were OK. I needed to do that before taking up my own position and saying: "OK boys, let's go." My most lasting memory of that day was when we slow-marched down towards the waiting hearse, passing the families. We were hit with what felt like a wave of grief.'

Conscious that there would be media interest in the return of Sasha's ashes, Kenneth's friend and colleague Mark Atkinson took responsibility for taking them from the crew of the C17.

'It was quite a moment,' recalled Mark, 'surreal in every way. There was my mate's coffin being carried off the plane and there was the shell casing containing Sasha's ashes. It didn't seem that long ago that I had seen both of them enjoying life. I know it happens, I know it's what we sign up for and I accept this can happen, but when it's your mate …

'We were conscious that there were two guys coming off the plane that day so we needed to be sure that the unprecedented arrival of a war dog didn't detract from what was really going on. But we needed to make sure that Sasha's repat was suitably solemn and conducted with full military honours, too. I took her ashes to our base in North Luffenham and placed them where we could all go privately and pay our last respects to a faithful and devoted friend. The shell casing was draped in a Union flag, just as her master would have wanted.

'We are soldiers but we are dog people first, and seeing Sasha's ashes was, I have to admit, heartwrenching. There were tears, and lots of them.'

Ken's Number 2s – his dress uniform – was brought in and handed to the undertaker for the funeral, but before that Mark put one MWD (Military Working Dog) coin in the top left pocket. The coin was one of only 100 specially commissioned by Frank Holmes to mark the closure of the Army Dog Unit in Northern Ireland and the transfer to North Luffenham in 2007. All staff and handlers received one, and Ken Rowe took his with him to the end.

THE FINAL R AND R

Lance Corporal Kenneth Rowe was home. Ironically he had left his FOB a day earlier and so landed a day earlier than his planned R and R had been due to take place.

Just five days ago his family had been making plans to meet him at RAF Brize Norton, straight off the 'Helmand taxi', and drive him back home to his beloved Newcastle upon Tyne. Home to one of his mother's famous roast dinners, or maybe he would have requested curry made to his Chinese grandmother's famous recipe. It was anyone's guess what Kenneth would have asked his mother to cook for him after four months of craving home comforts and home cooking.

Home, family, Newcastle United and dogs were everything to Kenneth. And now he had made his last journey back to everything and everyone he held dear.

LYN

After Iain Carnegie and Major Ham left I was probably still on another planet. The planet of disbelief. If ever there was a time that I was grateful for being part of a big family it was then. Having my brothers and sisters around took the pressure off Ken and the girls too and gave them another source of comfort.

It was natural that we would get swept up in the whirl of military 'must dos' and in a way I was grateful for the rigid procedure of it all. There was no opportunity to slope off and pretend it wasn't happening because there were things that had to be done and truths to face. And the one I dreaded most came first.

Repatriations were something other service families had had to endure. It was the flag-draped coffins of other people's sons and daughters we saw on the television as they drove through Wootton Bassett. We always watched with a lump in our throats, but from a position of comfort. Not now. Now it was our turn.

We had been told that there could be seven family members present but I decided that it would be enough to have the four of us. That's the downside of the big family – someone would have to be left out. This way everyone would understand and I wouldn't have to feel guilty. I just wanted to get my son home now and do everything as he would have wanted it.

Kenneth was just twenty-four years old when he died, and who at that age would have talked about their funeral? It wasn't something I had ever wanted to do with him, but in the days that followed his death I wished I had seen the sense in having that conversation. Iain Carnegie and Kenneth's Army friend Mark Atkinson had been given the unenviable task of emptying his room at North Luffenham, but they said they didn't find anything that resembled a last letter. Nothing that mentioned his final wishes, should anything happen to him on tour. I had hoped there would be something, something he wanted to say to us should the time come.

The Army recommends that soldiers put their lives in order before they leave on a tour of duty: make a will and write a letter or a series of letters to family and loved ones expressing their final wishes. The 'admin' letter is a thing of comfort to many, and in those days after Kenneth's death I needed that comfort so very much. Everything had happened so quickly and decisions had to be made blind. It wasn't so much to do with the repatriation, as that was in the hands of the Army and the RAF, but Kenneth's funeral had to be organised, too. Which songs would he have liked played? Would he have wanted prayers? Did he want hymns? How would I know?

I couldn't deal with that ahead of the repatriation. It was just too much.

We were driven to RAF Lyneham in silence. I don't think any of us knew what to say. Jeni and Steph were in pieces and I was afraid it would be too much for them, maybe too much for all of us. Ken was being his stoic self and I was relieved because if he had let emotion get the better of him I would not have been able to hold back. We all looked to him for strength and he managed to find it for all of us.

I don't recall much about the journey but I do remember the crowd of people gathered when we arrived. I didn't recognise many faces, and everyone blurred a little. The military guests and the family of the other soldier, Jason Barnes, outnumbered us but we had each other and I felt I needed to be strong for them as well as myself.

We were all seated formally to watch the C17 arrive. It was a beautiful day, clear skies and sunshine. Kenneth would have loved it. Suddenly we heard the deep roar of what sounded like a very large aircraft in the distance and it rumbled away for a while before it eventually broke through the clouds. Its rather menacing black shape entered the blue sky and seemed to stand still for several seconds before the pilot dipped its wings and levelled off for landing. All around me the sound of pain and tears began. I felt for Jason Barnes's mother. I shared her hurt and inside I was screaming too but I just could not let it out.

The ramp at the rear of the plane was lowered and the heat haze rippled the scene as the bearing parties were sent forward to bring out the coffins. The REME lads marched Jason away first and then Kenneth's coffin was lifted high on the shoulders of the RAVC party and taken slowly down the ramp under the watchful eye of Iain Carnegie. The slow march past us towards the hearse was the moment I could have let go but my daughters were sitting either side of me and I was holding their hands. If I had let go I would have let them down. I felt I needed to stay strong for everyone.

We were told we had to stay in our seats but the urge to run to Kenneth was hurting me. He was there in front of me but I couldn't hold him. It was a torture. I tried to detach myself from what I was seeing and how I was feeling. I didn't want to believe that the coffin that was being carried towards the hearse contained my son. Watching the hearse drive away from us was excruciating.

There was then a short time to collect ourselves before being escorted to the Chapel of Rest. I had already prepared myself for this nightmare – well, at least I thought I had. I longed to see him but the casket was closed so the best I could do was lay my hand on the top, close to his head, and speak to him. I knew I wouldn't be able to wake him for his breakfast, or tell him to hurry up or he'd be late for the match, and he wouldn't say, 'Don't worry, Mam.' I had to hold on to my girls and Ken held on to all of us. I remember Martyn Thompson saying Kenneth looked as if he was sleeping. I wondered if that was right. If that really could be true. I wondered if it was really possible to cry forever. It certainly felt like it.

By this time I think the day had turned into a haze of spent emotion. So much so that the journey to Wootton Bassett seemed very surreal indeed. Of everything that we went through that day the journey through the small market town and the sight of the people lining the route was the part I had dreaded the most. We had watched this scene so many times on the television, almost holding our breath, because it was someone from the Army family being honoured and a family suffering. I didn't think I could bear it. As our driver started the journey through the town he asked if we would like to get out and watch. I'm pleased that I said yes.

The number of people lining the route was staggering. Dogs and handlers were amongst the crowd, which had to have included hundreds of people. We didn't have extended family with us so these people were strangers, but somehow it didn't feel that way. As I stood drinking in the incredible scene I remembered that all this started as a voluntary gesture by the people of the town. They didn't have to do anything to acknowledge the frequent passing of hearses carrying coffins draped in Union flags, but they chose to turn out as a mark of respect and to help the families say their goodbyes. Kenneth would have liked to see the dogs line the street, not just the military dogs handled by colleagues but members of the public with their pets. I'm sure Sasha would have liked that, too.

On the day that Ken Rowe and Sasha were repatriated to the UK, the RAVC and the wider Army were well aware that the loss of man and dog would rekindle memories of the four dog handlers lost to terrorism in Northern Ireland during Operation Banner. They were understandably sensitive to the public's reaction to the loss of Ken and Sasha, and although it wasn't a secret that the dog's ashes were being repatriated to the UK, it was an unprecedented situation. The handlers wanted it and they knew Ken would have wanted it. It had to be done and done right.

The day brought another poignant moment for me. Just after the C17 had turned off its engines, the RAF padre, who was standing close to the tail where the engines ticked and cooled, suddenly looked down and started to shift on the spot. Fluttering and dancing around his legs were two cabbage white butterflies. Darting and doing loop-the-loop, they didn't seem bothered that they could be brought down by the heat pouring out of the engines. They reminded me of two people who could not be there in person that day – my mother and my son. In Chinese culture the butterfly is a symbol of rebirth or reincarnation. Some won't believe in such things, but I do. I believe the butterflies were either Kenneth and his grandmother or maybe Kenneth and Sasha reborn and brought together again, and it made me smile to see them there.

I remember watching them and thinking, 'Stop it, Kenneth. Stop messing about!' But I was pleased to see them together because I knew that my mother would be looking after him and he wouldn't come to harm. I spoke to the padre afterwards and he said he was totally shocked to see butterflies at the tail of the plane.

He had never see it before. Nothing normally comes anywhere near, not even birds. He admitted that it spooked him but I hope my explanation helped. I know that every time I see a butterfly I think it must be Kenneth enjoying his freedom and happily looping-the-loop for eternity.

I'm sure I made it home before I allowed the full trauma of the day to take over. But I knew I couldn't go that far down because it was only a few days to go before the funeral, which was set for 8 August. Without a final letter from Kenneth we had nothing to go on so we were pretty much making it up as we went along. All we could do was do what we thought was best.

We agreed to a full military funeral – but it had to be with certain additions and I was not going to compromise. The Army padre was very patient with us and happy to conduct the service as we directed but, after hearing all we had to say, he did admit that it was a bit 'unusual'.

All we were sure of was that Kenneth would want a Bon Jovi song included, so we chose 'Livin' on a Prayer' and hoped we had it right. I turned to the girls for inspiration on another song and they suggested his favourite, 'My Immortal' by Evanescence. Somehow I knew that he wouldn't want to go down the religious route too far, so the readings were a mix of Scripture and poetry. My sister Jann wrote a poem about

Kenneth as a boy growing to a man, then a soldier. It was very touching and if there was anyone who didn't know Kenneth they certainly knew him after hearing the poem. The padre was happy. All he asked was that we didn't sing along to Bon Jovi!

Two days before the funeral I received word from the RAVC that a letter had been found with Kenneth's belongings that had been returned from Camp Bastion. Iain Carnegie had been asked to check the kit back in against the itinerary and there, between the pages of Kenneth's favourite book – *The Golden Compass* – was his last letter. He had been using it as a bookmark. It was in a pretty tatty state, or at least the envelope was as it had been roughly fashioned out of a single sheet of writing paper and held together with strips of tape. Written on the outside:

'For the eyes of Lyn Rowe only.'

When I held that letter for the first time I knew that, to me, it was the most precious thing in the world. It had been folded over a few times to make the perfect bookmark and it looked well travelled, as if he had kept it with him and added to it as he went along. As I unfolded it I wondered why he hadn't left it at Luffenham as he was supposed to. I suspect he had talked himself out of writing a 'death letter' but once he arrived in Afghanistan it suddenly seemed like a good idea and he had changed his mind. It was like every one of his letters – short on punctuation and full of 'original' spelling. It was the most beautiful letter I'd ever read.

> Hey Mum, Dad. Well what can I say really? I ain't that good at this type of stuff prob because I don't think this way.
>
> I haven't left a final letter with work back in North Luffenham but hey, I've just had a funny feeling. I was putting it down to slightly first time nerves like but as you're reading this my time was up and Mam, you're not the only witch in the family. Kidding aside for a moment.
>
> Mam, Dad, remember that I love you both so much it's untrue. Without your help, guidance, support, all of that what you two called parenting, I'm sure a lot of parents would not put up with the things I've done, said etc., over the last 24 years. Please believe me when I say I'm truly grateful and proud of having such good parents. Jeni and Steph will back me up saying that no matter whatever happens and what we say to each other we are such a close nice loving family that when it boils down to it we are there for each other.
>
> Don't be upset plz at what has happened. There isn't really anyone to blame apart from me really, I signed up for this and on the whole enjoyed it …

I know you'll want to give me a proper send-off so nothing too religious please. I know I was christened but it's not me all that god stuff. I want the dogs to be there and my friends in fancy dress but no red and white allowed! I want Bon Jovi's 'It's My Life' to be played and Nickelback's 'Rockstar'. That would be mint! … And you can tell everyone that it was great to be a part of such a good strong family.

(My son's letter then goes on for two pages with personal messages for each member of the family.)

So … Everyone enjoy yourselves, life is without doubt too short, live life to the full. Have a laugh, it's exactly what I would have wanted without a doubt. I hope I have done things that will always make people smile 'cos memories are the most important things I can ever think about.

Mam, I know I've been an ass and a dick at times. Hey, I've got a little tear in my eye … so I'll say … Stay safe, stay strong, especially as a family – we are so special as a family that people would give or should want to give anything to be part of it …

All my love as always,

Kenneth Michael Rowe xxx … Love you

The letter was written to me but there was something for everyone. Typical Kenneth to include his family members. He didn't forget the pets, either – his dog K and Trevor his tortoise.

I was relieved to see that we only needed to change the Bon Jovi track, so no major changes to the order of service at the eleventh hour. But I had to read on. I wanted to know that he had been happy and that he had thought about his life and his future.

I was pleased that we had been on the right track with the funeral arrangements and relieved that he didn't want anything too religious. I had fallen out with God. If there really was a plan to all of this I still couldn't understand why my son had been taken. He had only just started his life. As I looked through the albums of photographs to select a few for the order of service I saw a bright-eyed little boy always with a smile on his face. A boy who had dreams.

Kenneth was born on a Sunday (9 October 1983) and he was a child who lived out the words of the traditional rhyme as he was a good, bonny and happy baby.

Even from a very young age he was always up to something and I needed eyes in the back of my head to keep track of what he was up to. At the age of four he decided he wanted to be a mechanic like his dad and so for his birthday we gave him his own set of mechanic's overalls – he looked every inch the part. As he did with everything later in life, Kenneth took the role very seriously and was soon waving spanners around and causing mayhem.

By the time he went to school it was obvious to me and to his dad that our Kenneth was going to make his presence felt – and not necessarily for good things. Certainly the teachers would have their work cut out. Always the joker in the class, Kenneth liked to take advantage of the odd times that the teacher left the class unsupervised. One day his timing was a bit off and his teacher returned sooner than expected and caught Kenneth 'mooning' at her.

A swift trip to the Head's office ended with him being suspended for the day. Of course I knew nothing about this but I could tell from the look on his little face when he got home that something was wrong. 'What happened today, Kenneth?'

Assuming he had been rumbled he replied: 'Aw, man, the school's called you, haven't they?'

'No, Kenneth, they have not, but now I know there's something up so, come on, spill it!'

He couldn't help laughing. 'Mam, how do you always manage to do that? You always know when I've done something wrong. I'm sure you're a witch!' Then he told me what he had done wrong and that he had been suspended for the day. The following day the Head called me and asked me to go into the school with Kenneth so he could apologise to the teacher and explain that he was actually mooning at his mates, not her. He was allowed back into school the same day.

No one could ever stay mad at him for long. His cheeky Geordie smile and sense of mischief were a winning combination for Kenneth, who could usually sweet-talk himself in or out of anything. He had a gift for getting on with people and talking them round, which was to pay off later in the military. But he had another gift, too – with animals.

He was always bringing some kind of creature to the house, leaving his dad to build a cage or enclosure for the new pet. Frogs, birds and beetles were all brought home at some stage, and if they were limping or sick all the better – he would always nurse them back to health. Some of his 'patients' recovered too well, as happened with the very prolific colony of stick insects. Hoping an old fish tank would make a good temporary enclosure for these new pets, Kenneth popped them into their new home with a bunch of privet from the next-door neighbour's hedge and fixed a net over the top. The next morning the net had shifted and the stick insects had escaped all over the house. Whenever we heard the girls scream we knew the stick insects would be to blame.

Kenneth also had a Houdini-like hamster called Smokey. We never did find out how he managed to escape from his cage but he did it several times a week and always headed for the same place – my pillow – for the night! Pet dwarf hamsters Beardsley and Shearer lived a charmed life, too. Whenever Kenneth shouted, 'Aw, Mam, Beardsley's out again!' we knew what to expect. Fortunately the pair were as nippy as their namesakes so they always managed to avoid the jaws of Zuki the cat, but only after a mad cat-and-mouse chase round the house with Kenneth in hot pursuit!

It was my father who was responsible for encouraging Kenneth to have a dog and who talked to him about the Army. Dad had been in the Signals and enjoyed a good career so the role model of animal lover and soldier was already there. Kenneth used to go to my parents' house after school and my father would show him how to feed injured birds and nurture them until they could be released back into the wild. He took the dog – a long-haired German Shepherd – for walks and packed away all the knowledge he could about looking after dogs. Dad would often remark on Kenneth's gift with animals. I'm sure that's where the seeds were sown.

For his sixteenth birthday Kenneth wanted a dog, and it was hard for us to say no because he had done everything we had asked of him to prove that he was capable of looking after one of his own. He knew what he wanted: a German Shepherd puppy. So we did some research and found a reputable breeder and went to have a look at the six puppies in their litter. Kenneth made his choice. I wanted to know why he chose that particular puppy: 'Because she chose me ...' Kenneth had his first dog and she had picked him by rubbing her nose on his feet! He called her 'K' – just the letter K because, he said, he couldn't spell so best keep it simple!

K would do anything for Kenneth. She was very much his dog and he trained her well. He even taught her sign language: she could recognise his sign for stop and toilet as well as all the usual commands like, stay, come and sit. When she was ill he sat with her and fed her with a spoon, and over the weeks and months the bond between the two of them grew closer and closer. We all witnessed how K cemented his love of dogs and his ability to successfully train her to do just about anything he wanted.

When he announced that he wanted to join the police it was no big surprise. But when they rejected him because he was too young it was a massive blow. Kenneth, the boy with the big dreams of becoming a policeman, was not happy. He carried on with his job at Asda, collecting the trolleys, serving on the tills, customer service and security, biding his time until he could go for his second interview with Northumbria Police, only to be turned down again. At twenty years old he was still considered too young.

Kenneth had a foul temper. It wasn't seen that often but when it flared up everyone knew about it, and then, just as quickly, it was gone. He had reached his own conclusion: 'If the Police don't want me, the Army will.' He was right. When he came home from the local recruitment office he said they were sending him to Edinburgh for a fitness test and then they would see what they could offer him after that.

If there was one thing my son loved as much as dogs and his family, it was sport. Over the six weeks on the course he must have been tested at almost every sport known to man. Football, athletics and rugby would have been the ones he enjoyed the most, but if they had asked him to play golf or go fishing he would have shown how much he enjoyed those, too. After his disappointment with the police we were very pleased and proud that the Army not only passed him in all the tests but also gave him an award for his physical fitness.

The Army wanted him. Three units approached him with an offer to join: the Military Police, the Parachute Regiment and the RAVC. He was tempted to join the MP but the chance to work with dogs for a living was, in Kenneth's eyes, too great an opportunity to miss. The police's loss was the RAVC's gain and I had a happy son with a career mapped out ahead of him.

As I looked through the photographs for the Order of Service I wanted to choose ones that showed my son as he grew from boy to man. The baby, the toddler with his sisters, the boy, the man, the dog soldier – all smiling. Kenneth was always smiling, always the cheeky Geordie. I could not believe the photographs I was setting aside were for his funeral. But then I remembered that he died doing the job he loved, the job he chose to do and we were so proud of him. I remember asking him why he was a dog soldier and he said to me, 'Mam, what other job could I do that would put a smile on my face in the morning and it would still be there at the end of the day?'

We decided to hold Kenneth's funeral at St Bartholomew's Church in Longbenton, not far from our home. My parents are buried there and I hope that's where we will all find our final resting place so that we can all be together again. Although I fell out with God for a while over losing Ken I still hold true to the belief that we will all be together again, and so the family plot makes perfect sense.

It isn't pleasant thinking about death and funerals – we all try to avoid it if possible – but in August 2008 we had no choice but to face up to losing Kenneth. The best we could do for him now was get it right. At that time we had no idea the extent of the injuries Kenneth had suffered. To us he was home, but for the Army the next duty after the repatriation ceremony was the autopsy. And the thought of that was too much to bear. I was fighting thoughts of what really lay beneath the hand I had placed on the casket at the Chapel of Rest. And now I had to do the same thing again – for the final time. As I approached the closed casket I imagined him there, peaceful in sleep, but I could not hold back the other thoughts – the horrors running in my mind.

I wanted Kenneth to wear his Number 2 dress uniform and have his kit with him. He was to be buried with full military honours so it seemed right somehow. And I wanted to put a little gel in his hair. He never went anywhere without hair gel, so he wasn't going to make his last journey without it either.

There was to be a strong military presence at the funeral and there was a certain reassurance in that. And it meant there were things we didn't need to worry about, such as the firing party and the bearers. Iain Carnegie was again in charge of the bearer party – the same men who had borne Kenneth at RAF Lyneham would carry him into our church. Major Chris Ham would read the eulogy. Everything was in place, from the RAVC top brass to the music of Bon Jovi. We were ready to see our boy home.

'Heart-breaking' is the only description I can give to that day. I really felt my heart could break into a thousand pieces. Our lovely old church was full to capacity. Crowds were gathered outside. I could hardly believe it and I was grateful that people had taken the time to come and pay their respects, but I was equally relieved that we had decided on a private cremation at another location. I wanted to say my final goodbye in private. After everything that had happened and everything that we had been through in the fifteen days since hearing the news, Kenneth was still my son. MY son. And to be honest, I just couldn't find any more of myself to share outside our family.

Then for the first time in a big way I realised that I had forgotten something really important. I felt a pang of guilt because I had underestimated the level of grief that Kenneth's friends would be feeling. After all, they were his 'other' family, his Army family. I looked around the packed church and saw so many of the young women and men in uniform, in tears or holding back their tears, and I felt for them. They had lost Kenneth, too.

Although it was a private cremation for the immediate family the Army representatives attended too and we were happy that Major Ham and Iain Carnegie were there as they had known Kenneth well. They had seen him enlist as a boy and helped shape him into the dog soldier he became. They were clearly feeling the pain of the occasion and I felt for Iain particularly as he had found Kenneth's final letter and that must have been quite a shock. He would have known that he had found something extremely important that would mean everything to our family. Kenneth would have wanted him there and we knew that both men were there for us, too.

I sat and listened intently to the eulogy read by Major Ham, and although I didn't want to believe we were at my son's funeral the words were so wonderful and Kenneth would have loved to hear how much his work as a dog soldier meant to everyone else. He loved his job so much. I felt his words hit home as if Kenneth was in the room and I truly believe they left a stain on my heart.

What was so hard to accept was that we were all there saying goodbye to someone whose life had only just begun.

Chapter 7

Letters home
– Lyn

I could always tell when Kenneth was unhappy because his letters gave him away. If he was happy he would be all chatty and newsy and asking for all kinds of treats things to help him and Diesel be more comfortable. When he was unhappy I would read the letter and picture him sitting in the dirt, knees raised, writing paper resting on his legs. I could feel his words. I know he enjoyed a good whinge and moan, but then who doesn't? The thing is Kenneth's moans didn't last long. Once he had let them out, they were gone.

I remember one of the letters he wrote to me in April, about a month after he arrived in Afghanistan. It was a great letter because he had written it in diary style. It took me, it took us all, to a dirt hole in Afghan. I was with Kenneth and 3 Para in the desert. He took me through two days from the early morning into the night, so I knew when he was sleeping, washing, feeding Diesel, watching DVDs, waiting for things to happen and thinking of home. For the first time I saw a side of my son that really didn't get a chance to materialise day-to-day at home, in Newcastle.

For someone who I don't think ever bought a pen, Kenneth suddenly thought it was worth mentioning the bargain price of the pens and paper he was using. Very funny, as he was always taking my pens and paper and never thinking about the cost! And asking me to pass on the letters he sent to other members of the family, asking me because 'it's good manners', because as Kenneth would say: 'I was brought up, not dragged up!' It was nice to know that some things I had said stayed with him, even in the desert thousands of miles away.

Saturday 19 April
07.50hrs: Breakfast was a boil-in-the-bag sausage omelette and beans with another really shite cup of tea …

08.05hrs: The temperature's really starting to pick up now so will write more later … By the way, I'm starting to like drinking water now without the cordial. Honest! Mam, tell Dad we might have to get a fridge in the garage with one of those water dispenser thingies for when I get home. Now that's what I call proper English, like!

10.20hrs: Hi, back again. Just been mortared. Two mortars missed the location by 100–150 metres. The Taliban really should practise more, plus the bastards woke me up! It's really hot now … even in the shade. That's all for now folks! xxx

I'm back again … We have to stand-to every night and morning at 05.05 and 19.10 just in case the Taliban decides to attack – 200 squaddies with 40 vehicles, 10 .50-calibre machine guns, 10 grenade launchers, let alone about 10,000 rounds of 5.6s, but, hey, that's the Army for you!

It's long days here but some are longer due to not moving around a lot. Can you and Dad remember a picture I sent Dad on his mobile of my lil room on exercise? Well, this is worse than that. Ha! Ha!

Dug in about two feet with three rows of sandbags stacked up. Desert basher on top to give me and Diesel some protection from the sun. Got my roll mat that's broken and won't inflate and my sleeping bag then my Bergen to one side with my rifle and body armour positioned for easy access. This is my home.

Sunday 20 April
06.00hrs: Good morning Afghanistan! I've been asleep for four hours, just went to the toilet, picked up my daily rations and to my amazement at 06.35 some guy came round to my

little house on the prairie and handed me two parcels … I think they have been sitting here a while. That's what happens with all the moving around. I will make sure you have the right addresses as far as I can. Love ya! xx

07.30hrs: That's scoff eaten, baby-wipe wash done, teeth brushed, parcels opened, letters read and all packed away in my Bergen … waiting out on either another attack or orders to go and do some real work … meanwhile I've got a small fascination with reading. I'm onto *The Golden Compass* a second time and it doesn't ring true with the film, which is such a pity …

Tell Steph to hurry up moving out so I can have my old room back. Ha! Ha! Only kidding really … Talking *The Golden Compass* again. It's the only book I've got with me. I left Jeremy Clarkson's at Bastion.

08.12hrs: Me again. Hey, who else would it be really? I was just going to read chapter eleven of *The Golden Compass*, after cleaning my rifle, and wondered what kind of daemon I would have. Then I thought, well, I have Diesel with me so perhaps he would hold my soul and be my daemon? I wonder if other people would think a dog would be the right daemon for me.

10.10hrs: I'm fed up of the desert now. And I'm really pissed off. The 3 Para lads asked me if there was anything I needed as they had to do a run to pick up rations, water and ammo. All I asked them for was dog food. So what did they forget? Yes, the f'ing dog food!! I've only got enough now to last me until tomorrow. It's f'ing shite and it really pisses me off. I have enough in my kit to sustain him for another two days but it ain't the right thing to do or the best thing for him to be honest. Can't believe it's so hard to do something so simple. It's the British Army for f's sake!

12.30hrs: Sand storm now and has been for twenty minutes. Kicks in dust from everywhere and covers everything. Diesel's water bowl is already full of wet dust. Quite fitting that I'm having such a problem with dust as I'm reading *The Golden Compass*! I wonder who has the most problems with dust – me or Lord Asriel? Ha! Ha!

I'm hiding in my doss bag with a head torch writing this and waiting the storm out. D is curled up in the corner with my second basher draped over him to keep as much off him as possible. Hopefully it won't last much longer. xxx

15.30hrs: Well I fell asleep in the storm and woke about an hour ago. It went really hot but it has clouded over again now so bet it will rain next. Very gloomy. Still no work and told not moving anywhere until the 24th (April) hopefully getting a hele back to KAF.

Christ this sandstorm keeps coming and going and it's just been pissing down. And we've had some thunder and lightning which would probably have been pretty dramatic without the sandstorm at the same time! I've blocked my basher up to try and prevent as much wind and rain coming in as possible – like that's going to happen!

17.30hrs: Just had my evening meal of chicken tikka, rice and a cup of crap tea. Got a Yorkie bar – it has to be sweets for pudding! That's what I miss most about Army life to civvie is being able to eat almost anything you want to eat without having your food dictated to you day in and day out. But I was just thinking how much I could down a good family Chinese or egg and chips with fresh bread … things like that.

Sorry my writing's gone all funny due to the sand clogging the end of my pen and Diesel trying to get between me and the wall and still trying to fit on my inflatable roll mat – which no longer inflates.

19.00hrs: OK, best go and stand-to as the Taliban are literally that brave that they will attack us head-on in a fire-fight!

21.00hrs: Hey just realised I'm on page 10 of this letter ... Now tell me I ain't just bored the tits off you?

What I would do for a cheese scone right now is not worth thinking about!

Six days to the planned push ... I hope it happens ...

When I read the letters back now I can see that Kenneth did a lot of growing up in Afghanistan. There's a seriousness on the page and over the four months it's there more and more. He mentions his favourite book, *The Golden Compass*, many times but I suppose there's a lot of down time in the desert so reading about a fantasy world where good is pitted against evil ... it was bound to make Kenneth think about the story in a way he probably never had at home. Whenever I read the letters over now I can see why the book provided some escapism from what was happening all around him. After all, who wouldn't have wished themselves somewhere beyond the sand-blasted hell of Helmand?

To me that letter was a window into Kenneth's life in Afghan and, reading between the lines, I think it says 'I miss you lot.' Even now I read parts of it and cry: the yearning for egg and chips, the concern for Trevor his pet tortoise, praising me for sticking with my swimming lessons and conquering my fear in the water. I loved him congratulating his dad for facing his fear of technology to write his first e-bluey! It was so Kenneth … in a letter … a moment in time. Him all over.

Knowing what I know now I read his last few letters in a different way to how I did in 2008.

I don't just read them, I search through them. I want to learn more and more about my son's life in the place where he died.

24 June

The air-con unit in my room has broken down and it's like a sauna. I could lose so much weight here … and more fucking vehicle searches today. We've searched 20+ vehicles entering the Camp … so I'll be glad I'll be getting out of here on the 27th June. I'm doing a new job in a FOB not that far away in Helmand Province. Don't worry, though, I've been training for this. It's a great opportunity really. There is some bad news, though; I've been told that I can't get my promotion as I'm not eligible until October or maybe January. That also pisses me off!

There might be a posting to Brunei coming up … but I've been asked to go to Germany in November. It's a three-year posting, if Poole or Hereford doesn't work out. Which one do you think I should do take?

Well that's my little rant over! I'll write and ring you tonight if Op Minimise isn't on that is. Love ya as always Ken xxx

3 July

Just a quick one – how is everything? Have you seen much of the baby? We talk and email and seem to be OK … Keep me in touch with how everything is.

Well, that's all I got to say. Will write when I'm established with my new lot. Take care. Love you loads as always. Ken xxx

By the way parents, how are you coping with the tour? I was told to ask. In daily brief they told us to check on our families as they can go through more stress and anxiety than we do. So are you OK with everything? Is there anything we need to discuss? Don't be afraid to ask what you think could be a delicate question. Just ask me.

Oh Mam, I need some decent toothpaste and another exfoliating mitt. I bought some toothpaste in the NAAFI [Navy, Army and Air Force Institutes – military camp shops] which was supposed to be Colgate but it tasted like shit. I swear the dust gets into the toothpaste too. By the way the mitts are really cheap in Morrisons. Mam, I don't know if I've ever said but I really like writing the letters to you and the rest of the family. It really relaxes me and I wish I had more time during the day for that. How's my handwriting – be honest? I hope my spelling's not too shite?

How's the baby? I've seen photos of her on MSN, her mum sent them, and we were talking but I couldn't see much of the bairn. Is she beautiful, Mam? Bet she is. Hope she's got our skin and my jet-black hair. Oh Mam, I can't wait to get home …

Love you as always. Ken xxx Rabb says hi too!

9 July
My R and R is cancelled so at the moment I ain't comin' home. Shite. My captain is on the case so I should get my leave as planned but I wanted you to know the score. I'm raging at the moment but what can I do about it? The decisions are made by people higher up than me.

Sorry about the camera. I was taking cover and didn't think about the camera. I hope it can be mended after all the trouble you went to find one for me and get it out here. It was a bloody lovely one too.

I've asked them to send Sasha out to me which means I'll be back on search dog work all the time. Andy Dodds has been working her in Garmsir and she was working well finding everything the Taliban put down or try to hide in the tunnels there. Andy's taking on a new role and he won't need her for a while so I feel comfortable about that. I'll be much happier when Sasha gets here. She's a bloody good dog … I'll be alright with her. And she's a light creamy coloured Lab, not golden like Diesel, so she will do better with the heat too.

Would love to have seen Jeni bath the dog! Mine and Jeni's relationship has shifted since I've been over here and I feel closer to her, more than I ever have before. I think my coming here has made the difference but I'm not sure if my siblings see that, but I know it's true! I like it.

On the R and R – just thought, I'm owed two weeks so I'm going to ask if they can be added to my Christmas leave which means I'll get six weeks at home. Can't wait!

Mam, have you seen much of the baby and her mum? Let me know how that's going will you? After this lot's over I've got some career decisions to make and it's on my mind.

One decision I have made in this life is I'm going to stop doing things for people who let me down. Well that's my gripe out of the way! Remember I love you all. Ken xxx

12 July

Hey hello there and how are we on this
ridiculously hot day in Helmand Province,
Afghanistan? Only eight days until the hottest
day of the year but here we are bloody boiling in
the day and blasted by sandstorms at night. It's
like thick blankets of sand just hitting you in the
face. We're covered in it all the time – the guys
and the dogs.

Mam do you think you could send some
cordial to put in the water? It's bloody
disgusting. I thought I was getting used to it but
I was wrong. It's shit but not as shit as the tea.
Could you send some proper teabags please? Aw
that'd be just great. A proper cuppa. I dream
about it.

Hey, I've got Sasha now and she's bloody
marvellous. I knew she would be. Captain
Thompson brought her out to me at Inkerman
and we got on right away. She's already made
friends with the guys of 2 Para. She's got a bit of
a reputation for being good at her job – just like
me eh???? So we're having some successes out
here and impressing the boss no end!

She has to be the best dog out here. Got to be.

There's a big push planned. Me and Sasha are
waiting to hear what happens next but we're
used to that. Meanwhile we're helping with the

planning for the job and hopefully we will get a lot of success on this one.

The internet has been down for a few days so sorry I've not been sending any e-blueys. It's not that easy here. One internet terminal and two text link terminals between 200 people doesn't really add up. It's different at Bastion where you can book time. It's not like that here. There's no booking time and with so many people waiting it's a check your emails, reply to them and then get off so someone else can have their turn. We all need that connection with home Mam. It means so much out here. It's a good for morale thing.

Did you manage to tape *Top Gear* for me? Please say you did? It's the only programme I try to watch religiously so I'm gutted I'm not in Bastion to watch it. I'll be catching up on all of them when I get home. Dad, what's happening with the Grand Prix? Who's going to come out on top?

Sorry Dad, no juicy news to tell you. I've been sitting in a FOB sweating my arse off. It literally is unbearable. My next holiday is going to be in Greenland in December I think. Sorry but I'm praying for rain when I'm home.
So 40 days or something till my 'original' R and R dates. I'll find out if that has changed

when I get to Bastion. I return there on the 20th or 21st.

Any news on how the baby is doing?

All my love, as always. Ken xxx

23 July

This bluey is just in case my text link isn't working as I sent you an email today (18th July) at around about 13.00hrs with regards to my bank card and my R and R. I need you to ask Barclays to send me my pin number. I know they won't give it to you but they can't send it to me by post here either. I can't ring them from here as I don't have enough minutes to go on hold. So when I get to Brize I won't have any money at all, not even for a phone call.

On my R and R date: if I get R and R at all it will be from the 20th to the 3rd, meaning I arrive at Brize on the 20th. My unit will pick me up and take me to Luffenham where I can pick up my number 2s but then I will need a lift home. I know it's a long trek that's why Dad might be the best to come. I've thought of asking Uncle Martin but trying to get in touch with that guy is harder than killing all the Taliban! I will pay petrol if needed and food etc on the journey. Dad's car would certainly be better due to diesel consumption. This needs to be resolved quickly as my R and R is fast approaching. I will let you know confirmed dates ASAP along with the timings. Let me know ASAP what's going on please. I don't want to be stuck anywhere.

Cheers Mam. Love you loads as always. Ken xxx

That was his last letter home.

I read it from time to time to remind me that he always intended to come home. Even if everything around him was out of his control and seemed ever so crazy, the one thing he was sure about was that he wanted to come home.

SIXTH SENSE

Out in Helmand on the morning of 24 July Ken Rowe had said to one of his colleagues, 'I've got a funny feeling about today. Something's going to happen.' But that wasn't an unusual experience for Ken. Like his mother, he had a sixth sense and often shared how he felt with his unit. One of his COs felt it was worth having a word with him about it.

'Ken, you need to stop saying things like that. The "we're all doomed" approach isn't a good attitude to have out here and it unnerves others, too. And you do know that if you keep saying it, chances are that one day you could be right.'

That day, Ken Rowe was right.

'I think up until 5.12pm on 24 July 2008 I had not grasped the full concept of what we and what I was doing in Afghanistan,' remarked Frank Holmes. 'Until that point it had been other people getting killed or injured. The flag was lowered for someone else's son, daughter, soldier, but when I was told that Ken Rowe had died that day my attitude changed completely.

'I asked myself, had we treated the build-up to this Operation, to this point, as a bit of a game? Just an adrenaline rush? I was gutted when Lance Corporal Craig Ide was involved in a mine strike on a patrol early in the tour. I was involved in one the very next day. Somehow many of us never thought anything would happen to us or those around us.

'Northern Ireland as I had known it back in 1992–4 was the place to be. We were training for a purpose – to defeat terrorism – and the pace of soldiering was fast and furious. But before the close-down in 2007 it was a shadow of its former self. It was down to the few like Ken Rowe who showed that keen desire to progress his dog, himself and his career in what was still a war on terror.

'Ken was one of our finest. And we lost him. Our standards needed to be raised and tailored to meet the new level of attack that we had to expect to meet. I tested and trained our handlers accordingly, including Liam Tasker.'

At the time when the RAVC lost Lance Corporal Ken Rowe, 2 Para were experiencing almost daily losses. They also lost a man in the same ambush. Herrick 8 was proving to be the regiment's toughest yet. The terror threat that faced them seemed to know no bounds. In a culture where life is cheap, where terrorists entice children to strap explosives to their bodies and die for their faith, the rule book is out of the window.

As the Taliban called the tune the pressure fell on the RAVC to turn the intelligence gained on the front line into dogs and handlers ready to locate the latest enemy devices. Liam Tasker was one of the trainers given the task of bringing good dogs forward and now he had the chance to go forward himself with Operation Herrick 13.

Chapter 8

Stay safe. Love you loads, son xxxx

Alongside the bearer party at Kenneth Rowe's funeral was a young Lance Corporal, Liam Tasker. His job that day was as hat orderly, collecting the bearers' caps, but the occasion overwhelmed him and placed in him a need to honour the fallen dog soldier, not at home, but in the heat and dust of Afghanistan.

JANE

Liam was always up to something and if he had a bee in his bonnet God help anyone who tried to stand in his way!

When he was deployed to Afghanistan in September 2010 one of the first things he noticed at Camp Bastion was the memorial to Ken Rowe. It stood at the entrance to the military working dogs' kennels – which had always had the unofficial nickname 'Muttley Lines', but in remembrance of Ken it was officially named

'Rowe Lines' in 2008. But for Liam that wasn't anywhere near enough of a tribute.

Liam rarely wrote letters, in fact I don't think he ever wrote me a letter. Yes, I had cards and the odd email, but Liam was a phone man and so I often had calls giving me the latest news, and if there was something bothering him I would know.

From very early in that tour I got the very clear understanding that Liam was, to say the least, very unhappy about the lack of what he would call a 'proper' memorial to Ken Rowe. When he told me that he had drawn out a design for a more fitting tribute I knew that, whoever his commanding officer was out there, they would certainly hear all about this new memorial every day until Liam had seen it built and dedicated. I couldn't help laughing to myself because that was typical of Liam. I often think that if people were dogs, Liam would have been a terrier – digging, chewing and pulling until he got what he wanted.

I remember how fired up and excited he was when he told me that he had mentioned his idea for a new memorial to a colleague and together they had come up with a design. It included a large dog's paw suspended by chains, all within a wooden framework. It sounded very ambitious to me and I wondered when on earth he was going to find the time to construct it, but I made all the right noises (I hope) and said, 'That's wonderful, son. You do that.'

I never thought of Liam as a handyman. If he had been building it with his dad, Ian, or his stepdad, Jimmy, I would have known that he would have had the right hammers and nails and whatever to do the job, but on his own it would have been achieved on pure energy and dedication. That was my son, Liam.

When Liam was first deployed I was on my laptop 24/7 just in case he was online. We 'chatted' as much as possible and I became so obsessed with looking out for him that Jimmy had a quiet word with me. He was worried that I would exhaust myself if I kept up that pace for the entire sixth-month tour! That's when I started writing the letters – every day.

Sometimes I wrote twice a day. It was my way of staying sane but I'm sure some of the letters must have driven him mad. Thinking about it now I'm sure that if anyone sat down and read all the letters I sent they would probably think they were the ramblings of a crazy woman!

Sitting in the Afghan desert Liam was subjected to the daily news of what was happening in the Duffy/Tasker household on the NATO base in Belgium, and that included news of the washing machine breaking down, his sisters Laura and Nicola doing their girly stuff, dance lessons, Brownies and the joy of a new television. It was all stuff that he would have been involved in if he was home with us so there it was in my letters. I know they made him laugh and I know he shared my stories with his mates, too – embarrassingly!

I don't know what possessed me but I remember telling him all about a woman on the TV quiz programme *Deal or No Deal* who messed up and lost £20,000 in prize money. For some reason, which escapes me now, her expensive mistake really got to me! I rattled on to him in the letter which he passed around his mates. I'm sure they all felt sorry for him having to put up with his mother's ranting and raving but it started the *Deal or No Deal* banter between us and from then on if that was mentioned it was Liam's way of telling me that I was 'going on a bit'!

For me writing a letter was the next best thing to having my son at home chatting away and bustling around the house. Liam always made me laugh. We never saw him show any anger but we remember his gift for laughter; even when things were far from funny he had a way of seeing the funny side. He always told his elder brother, Ian (we call him 'wee Ian' so as not confuse him with his dad) and his sisters that he was 'Mum's Golden Child'. They thought it was hilarious and it was that kind of cheekiness that helped him get what he wanted at home and it probably got him out of trouble in the Army, too.

Liam was always up to something and if I'd given birth to him first God knows if I'd have had any more children! He always had mischief written all over his face and his rosy cheeks and hazel eyes were always getting him stopped in the street. 'Oh, isn't he a little angel?' was something I heard very often, especially from elderly ladies, when we were out shopping. I remember thinking: 'If only you knew what a little demon he is at home!' His dad always said: 'Liam is a remarkable boy – for many, many reasons,' and I agree. Certainly he was a character and anyone who met him was unlikely to forget him.

Liam was born on 11 December 1984 at 1.15pm at Forth Park in Kirkcaldy. It was an induced birth and he was the smallest of my four children, weighing in at six and a half pounds. While Ian took care of our posting to RAF Gütersloh in Germany I stayed with my mother in Scotland. It was such a busy time and here was this lovely early Christmas gift. We were so happy. It's really difficult to try to put into words just what Liam was like as a little boy, but I'm smiling just thinking about him and the things he got up to. If I have one word that described my son from day one it would be 'cheeky'.

He was a really good baby although he always needed to be doing something. Liam was nothing like his big brother, Ian, who was quite happy to amuse himself playing with his toys and games. They were great pals but Liam needed to be entertained, otherwise he would look for something to do and inevitably get into mischief. He was my wee lovable rogue. When he was up on his feet he always liked to dance naked around the house wearing my boots – he's gonna love me for saying that! He always had his cheeky wee grin and if he got upset we knew he must have hurt himself as it was the only time he cried.

Liam was always taking his lead from big brother Ian, which usually meant that he tried to walk before he could crawl. When he was three years old he was fascinated watching Ian ride his bike up and down the road and decided that he was going to ride a bike too. You could see in his face exactly what he was thinking and as soon as he got the chance and a little bike of his own he taught himself to ride it and he was off! Sadly he didn't have a scrap of road sense, which made nervous wrecks of my neighbours every time they saw him out at the front of their house!

When Laura was born on 7 December 1990 Liam was so excited. He had hoped that she would arrive on his birthday but when he saw her he forgot all of that and happily told everyone at the Mess Christmas party that day that his little sister had been born and she was called 'Flora'!

Liam always said he was lucky having two dads. Ian and I split up when Laura was two years old but Liam always remained very close to his dad, who he called his 'Dad-Dad' and to his stepdad, Jimmy. Liam was eight years old when Jimmy and I married so he always had his family there as a constant in his life no matter which RAF base we were transferred to next. And when our daughter Nicola was born, in March 1997, Liam was such a proud big brother and fussed over her all the time.

He was such a loving and caring lad and even as a small child he would do anything for anyone. It started back then, him telling everyone he was my favourite and calling himself the golden child! But when his brother or his sisters were ill he would always want to be with them and make sure they were not alone or unhappy. If he could make them feel better by making them laugh, he would be there.

He was the same when he was older – very protective and caring when it came to his family. One time my friend and I went to surprise Laura while she was at Leicester University so Liam took it upon himself to come and surprise me, bless him. And when it was his grandma's 70th birthday he travelled for eight hours to surprise her! He was just that kind of boy who grew into that kind of man.

So very many boxes packed and unpacked over the years, one cramped and hideously decorated married quarters after the other, but Liam took it all in his stride. It was the life he knew and loved. Later, when he asked his Dad-Dad, 'When did you decide what you wanted to do?' he got the reply: 'I still haven't decided!' The writing was on the wall; the Armed Forces would call to him.

School to Liam was not so much a place of learning as entertaining. School was Liam's stage. At the time he started school we were living on the base at RAF Turnhouse, so his first school was Corstorphine Primary in Edinburgh. From day one he was a wee monkey but the thing that usually got him into trouble was doing kung fu. He was really into it, so there wasn't a moment anywhere when he wasn't trying to axe-kick or reverse-punch someone. Unfortunately, he was forever trying it out on his school chums and that usually got him into trouble.

His brother Ian was mad keen on football so the weekends were taken up with my big son doing that while Liam went to dance lessons. He was a right little Billy Elliot and the only boy in the class. He loved it and I'm sure if the Army hadn't welcomed him into the fold the smell of the greasepaint and the roar of the crowd would have lured Liam onto the stage instead.

It was Jimmy who introduced Liam to rugby. We were stationed at RAF Staxton Wold and living in Driffield, North Yorkshire, at the time and I can honestly say, from his first touch of the oval ball, Liam was hooked. From that time on, wherever we moved, Liam wanted to get into the rugby team, and each time he worked to improve his game. When we were posted to RAF Boulmer he played for Alnwick, which was a real proud moment for Liam and it all stood him in good stead for later when he was based at the Defence Animal Centre (DAC) and earned himself a place in the local Melton Mowbray team, the Nomads.

But it wasn't all about rugby and his other passion, mountain biking. When we were posted to RAF Saxa Vord on Shetland for a couple of years Liam attended the secondary school there and took a keen, and not entirely unexpected, interest in drama. When they staged their own production of the musical Grease they couldn't persuade any of the 15-year-old boys to take the role of Danny. But guess what? Liam said he would give it a go! He was so funny and the girl who played Sandi was about a foot taller than him. He was so proud of himself, bless him.

He was such an easy-going, lovable lad. I miss him so much.

Then the day came when he announced that he was joining the Forces, but we were a wee bit surprised that he chose the Army and not the RAF. He had grown up with the RAF and lived most of his life on Air Force bases all over the UK. Of course he took a fair bit of boy banter, but there was a strong Army influence in the shape of my brother. Liam's Uncle Richard is a major in the Army and, as one of Liam's idols, he obviously made an impression. And big brother Ian was tempted into the Army too, so it was only partly going against the RAF family tradition. He would have found it really funny, especially if it amused everyone around him, too.

I'll never forget when Liam joined the Army – it was September 2001. The news was full of the 9/11 terrorist attacks in the US but little did I know how that devastating link to terrorism would affect my family ten years later. I couldn't have allowed a thought like that into my head at the time. I was more surprised that Liam decided to join the Royal Electrical and Mechanical Engineers (REME) and not the RAVC. He loved dogs and although we were a Forces family, moving regularly from base to base, we did have a dog – Rags.

Rags was a handsome, mostly Border Collie with long legs, a smart black and white coat, and I swear he had a permanent smile on his face. He was just the kind of odd dog that Liam felt proud to call his own. Rags might have been the original 'underdog' but he was wily enough to realise that he would be OK if he tagged along with us. So he did just that.

To see Liam skipping along with Rags at his heel was quite a sight. Liam was as stocky as Rags was skinny but they ran in a similar way – with a slight skip in their step – and every now and then they would turn to look at each other. Wherever the one was the other would never be far away. They were such good pals and Liam would share everything with that wee dog, everything from his food to his bed to hours of his time.

He trained Rags to do all kinds of tricks, which of course Liam loved to show off to anyone he could pester to watch. I'm sure that dog knew all of Liam's innermost fears and secrets. I know we always say 'if only dogs could talk', but if they could I'm sure Rags would have stayed loyal to Liam.

Acting the fool was always a feature of Liam's character. He couldn't help it. It was all part of his 'life is for living' philosophy and why he did everything to the extreme. If Liam was doing something then he would do it well and make sure he enjoyed himself, which is just how he spent his six years as a vehicle mechanic with the REME. It was when one of his mates showed him a video of military working dogs being put through their paces that he discovered a branch of the Army he had never seen before and decided it was time for a new challenge. He transferred to the RAVC in 2007 and from day one of the training he was loving it.

'Hi, Mum, it's your golden child here! These bloody Army dogs are amazing. I can do this job: I like the dogs and they like me and I'm having a great time. The trainers are good guys and it looks like I can have a bit of fun here, too. I really think I could make it to chief trainer here, Mum. How's you?'

I can remember him now chattering away on the phone telling me all about the dogs and the trainers and how he was settling in at the Defence Animal

Centre (DAC) in Melton Mowbray. My son was happy. He was excited, like a little boy again, so that made me happy, too. There's that moment when you know your child has found their way in the world, and that's how I felt when Liam joined the RAVC – he had found his 'home' in the Army.

There are several types of military working dog and for the next three years Liam Tasker trained every type that the military and the emergency services needed. The DAC had a responsibility to produce high-quality, multi-role working dogs and Liam Tasker joined the team that trained them and, according to his peers, he trained all of them – the biters, searchers and trackers – extremely well. Everyone could see that he not only had a way with people but he had a way with dogs, too.

When Liam joined his arms and explosives search dog course he came under the watchful eye of Chief Trainer Frank Holmes:

'Liam was technically gifted and the dogs were an extension of the man. I saw Liam regularly over the four months that he was on his search dog course and he was being tested all the time. The final exercise, which lasted five days, was intense. The soldiers and dogs had to be ready for the task ahead of them because we knew what was out there.

'The thing is, when we lost Ken Rowe I lost one of my own. Ken's death brought it home to all of us that for our dogs and for our soldiers the loss didn't end in Northern Ireland after all. I wanted to make doubly, trebly sure that these men and women were competent enough to handle a dog in a hostile environment. There was no doubt about it, Liam Tasker had something special. He had what it took, but what I couldn't do was make him – or any one of them – invincible.

Liam made himself at home as a search dog handler and trainer at the DAC and soon gained the respect of his peers. 'There was something about Liam Tasker,' recalls Major Chris Ham, Liam's Commanding Officer at the DAC. 'He was always smiling and always ready and willing to go that extra mile for the dogs and his colleagues and there was something else about him – he had courage. He was never afraid to say, "Sir, we have a problem …" and have the nous to suggest a solution.'

Happy in his role and loving life at the DAC, Liam had found his niche in the Army and was progressing well not only as a trainer but as an exceptionally competent and confident handler. Problem was, he had all the success and experience of a dog soldier in theory but no genuine operational experience. As is the Army way when someone is settled, it signals a time to move on.

There was mention of Afghanistan.

Chapter 9

Take one soldier and his warrior dog

JANE

When Liam was told he had a chance to go to Afghan he knew he wanted to go but he had a few things niggling in his head: he loved his job as a trainer and didn't want to lose that at any price. As far as Liam was concerned that job was his future, no matter what happened in between. And there was his girlfriend, Leah Walters, a veterinary technician who was also based at the DAC. He didn't want anything to change with her either. I think he liked the feeling of being settled, at last. Going on ops was what he had trained for and trained the dogs for. Now it was his chance to prove himself in the theatre of war. I was so proud of him and relieved that he was happy in everything he was doing. It suddenly felt easy – for once.

As I said before, Liam was never one for letters but he always tried to catch me on email or call me whenever he could so I soon got to know that pre-deployment training was no basket of roses for him. But you know how it is when you want something so much, nothing is going to stand in your way and that was Liam's approach to getting fit to get out there.

Liam was a rugby player and he was built like one. He wasn't a sprinter, unless the chance to score a try was laid out in front of him, but he knew from his mates that patrolling as a handler in the Afghan desert was a far cry from a walk in the park. He had been told that at its worst it was hard dirt underfoot with enough surface rubble to trip a goat and none of this was helped by the great weight of the equipment they had to carry, and of course they had the dog, too. I knew Liam would be OK but he just needed convincing of that and that's where his mates came into their own.

'I remember asking Liam what he wanted to do in the future and I knew right away what his answer would be – to be at the DAC training police dogs. It was what he loved doing and he was good at it too,' remembers Warrant Officer II Geordie Cunningham. 'As he said, "Why would I want to get a search dog and go to Afghanistan to get killed?" He had a point, and the death of Ken Rowe was still on everyone's mind. There was no getting away from it. There's danger in the job we do. The dogs do it for fun, they see it as a game with a tennis ball as a reward, but we know that it's not. It's about trust and respect and you get that through the training, and that's where Liam was a perfectionist.'

Sergeant Major Adrian Davies deployed on Herrick 13 with Liam, but not before he had put his rugby teammate through his paces. 'I played rugby with Liam well before we served together so I was aware of his competitive nature. He probably thought I tortured him with all the runs and weights we did before we deployed and the 6am runs I made him do once we got to Bastion. I had to do it with everyone.

'What lay ahead of us was not only going to be hard going physically but it would be psychologically demanding, too. Patrolling with the infantry could mean a six-to-eight-hour stretch on foot in the heat of the day and in whatever weather Mother Nature wanted to throw at us when we slept in the desert at night. And there's the sheer weight of the equipment to carry – oh, and the dog to take care of, too.

'I hope he has forgiven me now for pushing him so hard. I had to do it and it was in his interests to fully prepare for what lay ahead. Liam Tasker was a perfectionist so he didn't do things by half and he was tough on himself, which is a good attitude to have in a job like ours. I was glad that we deployed together because it meant I could keep on his tail at Bastion. Besides, Liam was my "go-to guy" so he couldn't escape me!'

According to his friends, mud didn't stick to Liam Tasker. He was too likeable for that. Corporal Ryan

Earnshaw recalls the first time he met his pal Liam: it was in the bar at the DAC in 2007. Liam's first words, 'Hey, knob-head, get a round in!' were the start of a good and loyal friendship, and that was typical of the man who was known for swaggering into the Guard Room and cracking a joke without fear of upsetting people. 'A bit of a git,' was one term of endearment. 'Trouble … but in a good if annoying way' was another. He was everyone's likeable rogue. Especially his mum's. Funny thing is, his dog had the same reputation.

Theo, a nippy springer spaniel, was 17 months old when Liam first set eyes on him. Theo had been donated to the Army by a member of the public and very early in his basic training he showed signs of stardom. Typically, being a spaniel, he showed an aptitude for specialist search work and immediately started to gain a reputation as a good dog capable of great things in the field.

While Theo was building his good reputation, Liam was working on his. When he was posted to the DAC Liam quickly proved to himself that he had a gift for his chosen career. He decided against matching with a Vehicle Search (VS) dog and decided on an Arms and Explosives (AES) dog instead and was the first in his class to 'break' his dog, Rob; then he did the same with his second dog, Eddie. His friend Ryan Earnshaw was working with a spaniel called Milo whom he described as a 'nutter who came good', but when Liam set eyes on Theo several months later all he saw was a spaniel with a gift.

When Liam started his pre-deployment training Theo had already attracted a reputation for being an excellent search dog. Not only that but Theo had something about him; he had a swagger and a full-on character. He searched with eagerness and drive and everyone remarked on how this waggy-tailed sniffer dog did his job with an eye for perfection and a bit of sass and cheek on the side. When Liam saw him in action he made a decision – Theo would be his dog.

Theo worked as Liam worked, with precision and flair. The dog looked like he was enjoying himself, and with every 'find' his tail wagged all the faster. It was the reason why Theo had to lose his tail – it wagged so vigorously all the time that it kept hitting against things and it 'split'! As a working dog this 'split tail' was proving to be an ongoing problem. It was a difficult decision for the RAVC vets to take but considering Theo was bound for operational duty in Afghanistan, where he could be on duty for days in the desert, it was a decision that had to be based on what was healthier and safer for the dog.

Clearly Theo couldn't say what he thought about losing the damaged section of his tail but it was obvious to everyone that he could just as easily wag his stumpy tail as a swishy feathery one! When Theo wagged his tail his whole body wagged with it. The dog with the zest for life and success met the soldier with the same dogged enthusiasm and it was a match made in Heaven. Everyone could see that.

'If truth be told, Theo was a dog version of Liam. They were similar in lots of ways and that's probably why they made such a good team,' Ryan Earnshaw recalls. His own search dog, Molly, was good in Afghanistan but he believes that was because she worked more like a 'robot'. Theo wasn't like that. 'Theo was a real character. He made you smile just to look at him and he had that same Liam cheekiness about him, too. I didn't blame Liam for doing all he could to make sure the dog went his way and, to be fair, it was the right partnership. They just made hard work look so easy, and having a fully trained dog ready to hit the ground running was perfect for Liam. He not only wanted to get out there and get on with the job, he wanted to be the best, and Theo was ready for it, too.'

Everything happened so quickly after that. Liam knew the dog was good so he asked for him and got him for Afghanistan. 'They were a strong search dog and soldier team,' recalls Adrian Davies. 'Liam was a strong handler with a strong dog and as a member of a team he could also see through people right away, which is always an asset in the job. He also had the gift of the gab, which was bearable because he could always back it up! He liked a challenge and anyone who served with Liam will remember the significant finds competition and his "bragging rights". He always pushed the boundaries with his cheekiness and his lack of fear for authority. He never liked to lose so if he said his dog would call the most finds on a patrol then he would work to prove his point. Liam just liked having a laugh, but for all his bravado and jokey point-scoring he was always someone you could rely on. He would be there for you. No question.'

Out on the ground the partnership of Liam and Theo made an impact from the start. Sergeant Matt Jones had completed two earlier tours of Afghanistan before he encountered Liam on the run-up to Herrick 13. 'The first thing I remember about Liam was his eagerness to get in and get the job done. He was happy to roll up his sleeves and give the job all he could, and that's just what you need out on Ops. I got on with the man right away. It was hard not to. He was such a cheeky git.

'As for Theo, well, he was a great dog and you could tell that Liam thought the world of him. It just shone out of both of them. If Liam said his dog was the best then he believed it, and from my perspective, as a dog trainer, it was the combination of respect and high drive from the dog and dedication and intelligence from the handler that was going to produce the results.

That was very much the case with this likeable pair. You couldn't miss them.'

No two dogs are the same, and according to everyone who met Theo he was just a whisker away from extraordinary. Liam loved to brag about him and often told the story of his first find in Afghanistan. Ryan said Liam always took pleasure in recounting the story because it showed the greatness of the dog. The story goes that before joining the patrol Liam told everyone who would listen that Theo would indicate on his first patrol. Out only a few metres and he 'called it'. Theo had come through for him, and that happened again and again, with Theo notching up seven finds on that route. 'In your face, Theo!' Liam said, punching the air as the patrol returned to base safe and sound.

There's no room for over-sensitive souls in the Army and 'BLT' (Big Liam Tasker) always took the banter in his stride. But those who gave it always had to remember they could be at the sharp end of his wicked sense of humour, too. And the time Ryan decided to grow a moustache was the time Liam decided to make him regret it. 'I remember it well and I know I should have known better than to give Liam a chance to have a go, but it was too late once he saw my effort to grow hair on my top lip,' says Ryan. 'I knew I was in for a good verbal pasting as soon as he looked at me. "What the fuck is that?" he said, pointing. "Mate, that's not a moustache, that's a shit-tash!" and wiped boot polish on it. I hoped that would be the last of it but, oh no, it was there in the BLT repertoire of jokes. He even made his own "shit-tash" by glueing hair on his top lip! The man was a legend, I tell you. A bloody legend. He was larger than life, with a heart of gold. And Liam and Theo were meant to be together. They were absolute soulmates.'

If you are in the Army your fellow soldiers are not just part of your team, they can also save your life. In some respects life in the Armed Forces is similar to life in Civvy Street: obstacles get thrown in your way and the old adversaries – fear, loneliness and low self-esteem – are really only ever a heartbeat away. But if you have a good buddy to lift you when you're down and to inspire you to stay at the top of your game and in times of desperation inspire you to stay alive, then you are one of the lucky ones. For Liam Tasker the best bud of all was his Army pal, Theo. That's Military Working Dog: 8260.

Chapter 10

The man and his dog

My son Liam and his bomb dog Theo were so close you could hardly see where the one finished and the other began.

Liam was deployed to Afghanistan in September 2010 and I'm sure from the moment the last glass was emptied at the pre-deployment party I started to worry – just a little bit. His flight out was delayed a couple of times, so that had me on edge, and then as soon as I heard he had arrived I had to speak to him. I missed our chats and his silly sense of humour. Somehow writing to him every day filled the gaps and shortened the miles between us. If I wanted to talk to Liam I knew that I could just switch on my laptop or reach for a pen and a bluey. There was always a massive comfort in that.

Liam took his R and R in January and that was because he felt it would work better knowing he was near the end of his tour when he returned in February. He spent the first few days with his girlfriend, Leah, just settling back into life in the UK and chilling out.

He caught up with his brother in Milton Keynes and his sister, Laura, who was at university in Leicester. I was still in Belgium with Jimmy and Nicola but I couldn't wait to get back to Melton Mowbray where we stayed when Liam was on leave. It was magical to have him home with us again. It was just like old times – well, at first anyway.

There were all the usual 'in' jokes between Ian and Liam and then between him and Nic and Laura. I just stood back and listened to it all. I drank it all in like a good wine. The chatter and the laughter. Good heavens, we are a noisy lot! Then I see Liam with a big smile on his face, arms around the others, looking at me. After a wee while he breaks away from them and comes over to me. He stands close, towering over me, and puts his arms around my shoulders. He's such a big, handsome man now but also still my little boy. 'Thank you, son. I've missed you so much.' I had to say it although I'm sure he could tell.

We went out for a welcome home meal and it was just fabulous but I could tell Liam wasn't quite himself. Call it mother's instinct if you like, but I could tell that there was something in that faraway look in his eyes. He was restless. I asked him, 'What's wrong, son?' He told me that he felt bad knowing that there were people still out in Afghan doing his job and risking their lives while he was home enjoying his leave. That was typical of Liam.

He talked about his Army mates a lot, that was normal, but I think he was really missing them and the life out there. He liked being home but he also wanted to go back to Afghanistan. I had seen that look enough in my family over the years so I wasn't upset by it and, besides, he was a soldier after all. There was a job to do out there and he wanted to get on with it. Typical of the soldier in the man and typical of the attitude to duty. I knew I was right because I knew him better than anyone …

The leave was soon over and it seemed that in no time at all he was packing his bags again and heading for Afghanistan. When we said our goodbyes he hugged me so tight. I was crying my eyes out and could hardly speak. 'Come on, Mum, don't be silly. I'll be home in six weeks!'

By 3 February he was back in the desert and on constant patrol duties with Theo so he had to give in his phone. That's when the blueys came to mean everything to me. I wasn't sure if he was even receiving them but I had to write. I just had to. I swear I would have gone mad otherwise.

I was also strangely excited because I knew that he would be home again very soon and I know I kept asking Leah if she had any plans for when he came home and to let me know. I felt we were on the countdown to the end of him being away. I couldn't wait for the day.

In every communication home Liam would talk about Theo. When we spoke on the phone, which we did regularly, he would ask about everyone at home and update me on anything he was allowed to say from his side, but at some point in the conversation it would come back round to Theo.

Not a big spaniel or a chunky spaniel, Theo was definitely more a slim springer than anything else but there was a cross with something. He was a handsome dog: he was black and white speckled all over with one big, black spot on his back. His muscular legs were feathery and spotty and always on the move. When he wasn't running or sniffing around on a search his paws padded around on the earth like an impatient sprinter. His lovely chiselled features and smooth black head were very distinctive and his crinkled black ears seemed to stand out from the side of his head as if they were constantly on 'radar' duty. And he never stood or sat still. Even when he was ordered to, Liam said his dog found it impossible to be totally still. His bottom still shuffled a bit or his legs shook with excitement. He reminded me a lot of Liam in that way; always ready to move on to the next thing with an upbeat attitude of 'OK, so what's next?'

That dog was part of our family in every way: he received presents in the post from all of us and we always asked after him. Liam was given Theo just two weeks before they deployed to Afghanistan and I remember Liam saying how the bond with his dog was so quick and easy. By the time Theo had passed through his licensing they were working so closely that anyone would think they had been partners for years! We soon realised that if everything was good with the dog then little was going to be wrong with Liam. It was very much 'love me, love my dog', and his girlfriend, Leah, loved him for that, too.

Liam used to say, 'You know, Mum, Theo is one hell of a dog and a good mate, but the best thing is even after a full day searching in that heat he just wants to play and then stretch out on my cot or snuggle into my sleeping bag. He's always after the best spot and messes about like a really good mate, but he never asks me to stand him a pint!'

Liam was never short of friends. He was a fun-loving, outgoing boy and people just loved being around him. It was probably because he had a magical way of lifting people's spirits just by being around them or saying something daft to make them laugh. He really could bring sunshine into a room, and everyone who knew him misses that. I do. There was always a hug and a smile from Liam and somehow he could still manage to deliver all of that in a phone call from thousands of miles away.

We all need a best mate. I've certainly been glad to have my friends around me, especially over recent years, but out in Afghan I know from other mothers and other lads and lasses who've served out there that friends take on an extended role. Out there your mates don't need to just be the guys you mess around with on a Saturday night. Out on the ground there the people closest to you can mean the difference between your life and death, but of course Liam was lucky he had his best mate beside him every day, and very few soldiers could say that.

The challenges out there were great and I know there were times when Liam needed someone or something to lift him when he was down or doubting, someone to be the little voice in the background reminding him why he chose to do such an incredibly dangerous job and keep him focused and on track. Liam's best mate didn't swear, put scorpions in his bed or carry a gun, but he did offer lots of love and affection when it was needed most. Theo was Liam's best mate and everyone knew it.

'Mum, Theo's a little monkey! He keeps trying to get into my bed. I always let him lie there but when I tell him to move he moans and then it turns into a staring competition, then a growling contest, until finally he gets off the bed! He's a little sod but he's great, Mum, really great.' There's no doubt that the relationship Liam shared with Theo was very special and it was probably one of the reasons why the Army chose them to feature in a press call at Camp Bastion. It was a chance for the media to see and hear what war dogs are made of and Liam was over the moon to be asked to do it.

I remember that I was in my French language class when my friend's text came in telling me that Liam's photograph was all over the British press. Liam had mentioned briefly that something like this might happen but didn't say when. I was so excited and proud. Apparently I shrieked down the phone when I called all our friends and relatives to tell them. They've never forgotten it. Sorry, folks, I couldn't help it. Our Liam in the papers and on the telly too! I was literally jumping with excitement. He had done all he could to get out there and now he was the 'poster boy' for the Corps! I could have burst.

14 February
Happy Valentine's again!! How proud I am of you, son. I could burst with pride. Great photos and write-up in the papers. You have been busy haven't you? Just be careful OK? I've been showing everyone the newspaper cuttings and Nic has the news on in case you are on tonight. And I have too! I was told there was a wee write-up in The Sun so I went and bought three copies. Then when I saw the one with the picture in the Times I took them back and swapped them. Granny has been and bought some newspapers as well so no doubt the whole

of Dundee will have seen it by the end of the week!

I'll keep going online, I'm looking at it now … How sad am I??? Well, not really, just one really proud Mum. I'll bet it's cost you a few crates, eh son?

Dad, the big poof, hasn't been to work today. He has, wait for it … a bloody COLD! Can you believe it? I have too and a sore throat but I went to work. You will have to give him some stick son, lol!!!

Nic and I got you some bits at the GB today so will get those posted off to you tomorrow. Dad wants to get you some sardines so I will have to send another parcel in the week as the one I have is already 2kg. Just thought I'd better let you know so you can look out for them son. Will get Laura to send some peppermints and what have you from the UK and get them off to you. That will keep you going until you get back. If you want more of that cheesy pasta let me know and I will get Granny to get it. It looks like you can only get it in Scotland.

Gonna ask Nic to choose a photo of herself in her new dress so I can add it to this letter … back in a min … Back again. Hope you can see it now? You will see what I mean about her looking all grown up. Scary!

Now gonna print off some of those pictures of you in the papers. Will drop you a line tomorrow son.

Take care. Stay safe. Love and miss you loads. Mum xxxxxxxxxx

18 February
Hi Son,

Sorry, I didn't get a chance to write last night so you'll probably get two letters from me today! The thing was after work and having my tea I went bowling and then I was up early to catch the bus and it's well early for me – quarter to six. Afternoons are OK but not the mornings. I had good intentions to come back this morning and go for a run but it's so cold I'm gonna do my ironing first and see if it warms up any!

Awww, guess what my boss did for me yesterday, Liam? He saw your picture in the paper and went online and printed it off for me on photographic paper. Wasn't that nice of him? It's amazing the number of people that are sending me messages saying what a great job you are all doing. Even friends of friends that I don't even know! Can't tell you enough how proud I am of you son. Not that I wasn't before you went there, Lol. Oh, you know what I mean!

I see it's really cold out there. It's the same here and it's freezing again so I have to defrost the car every morning. I don't know what's going on with this weather.

I'm now on the countdown for you coming home and I can't wait!!! Mind and give me a date as soon as you have something definite son so we can get leave sorted. Gonna be well strange for you and the lads when you come back after being so busy! Make sure you keep your head down son. Not long now. Love ya!

Anyway … I've got that photo that my boss printed off for me in a frame. My house is gonna be like Granny's is with pictures of Uncle Rich all over the walls, lol!

Must go and do my ironing son. Will drop you a line tonight.

Take care. Stay safe. Love and miss you loads. Mum xxxxxxxxxxxxxxxxxxxxxxxxxxxxxxxxxxxxxxx xxxxxxxxxxxx

To be honest I kept writing and writing even though I didn't know what Liam was up to. Just that he was being kept very busy with his job. I learnt later that Liam and Theo had been supporting No2 Company, 1st Battalion the Irish Guards, since 19 February. His job was to locate IEDs and so save lives, not just of fellow soldiers but the local people, too. I remember someone saying that, at the time, more farmers than soldiers were being killed by Improvised Explosive Devices in Helmand. I suppose we don't always think of it that way. Certainly Theo was good at his job and Liam was very proud of him.

Some of the newspaper articles that appeared on 14 February (2011) were headed 'Theo the superhero spaniel!' and it was great to find out just how good Theo was. They said he held the record for finding the most IEDs and weapons in Afghanistan to date. As the 'front man' of the patrol Theo had notched up 14 operational 'finds' on his tour so far and Liam was so proud. I read what he said in the paper: 'I love my job and working together with Theo. He has a great character and never tires. He can't wait to get out and do his job and will stop at nothing.' I read it and knew it was also true of Liam.

The photographs in the paper and the footage they showed on the telly were so good. There we were, the rest of Liam's family, reading and watching on the base in Belgium, and there was my son and his dog going through their paces at Camp Bastion. It was quite something really and humbling in a way to see my son doing the job he loved so much. It was a real chance to show the world exactly what the dogs and the soldiers do on the front line. I could have burst with pride.

But then it hit me. There was a downside to the press coverage: Theo's success rate meant that he was to stay for an extra month after his tour had officially finished. Liam was due to end his tour in March and that meant he would be parted from Theo.

Liam called me on the Saturday – 10am in Belgium. I was attending an international Thinking Day with my Brownies. I was Brown Owl at the time and we were just about to take the girls on stage when my mobile rang.

'Hiya, Mother.'

'You all right, son?'

'You know I've been told I'll be leaving Theo behind when I come home? Like it said in the papers he will be doing an extra month out here. I don't like it, Mum. I know he's a good dog and all that but I want him to be there when I get back. I don't want to come home and then lose him to someone else. I'm worried, Mum.'

'Son, they're not going to split you two up. Theo is your dog but you'll have to put up with him working with someone else while you're home. You know how it goes, but then you'll be back together. Don't worry about Theo. He'll wait for you, son.' I changed the subject as he said he didn't want to talk about it.

'Are you on the countdown to coming home now, son?' I had to ask him but I hated hearing the response: 'Not yet, Mum, I've got another job to do and then I'll be back in Camp Bastion in a week.

'Mum? Can you get hold of Leah for me? I want to talk to her about plans for when this is all over. Is that OK, Mum?'

Of course, I said I would do that, and then I tried to cheer him up by telling him that the OC of the Army UK section had given me a bouquet of flowers. He laughed, saying he wondered what I had done to deserve something like that! We chatted a little while longer and then he said he had to go and would ring me in the week.

He was gone.

I didn't hear my son's voice again.

Leah spoke to Liam on the Sunday and fixed everything for when he was due home in a couple of weeks' time. The last letter of mine that Liam opened was returned to me later. It was dated Monday 28 February. A totally unremarkable letter in lots of ways, just me going on about the usual things. But of course it means a lot more than that to me now.

28 February

Hi Son, It was great to speak to you on Saturday and I'm glad you managed to get hold of Leah. That must have given you a wee boost! I noticed on Facebook that she has booked leave for when you are back. We definitely want to meet you and bring you home, son. We wouldn't miss it for the world!!

I went for a run today, the first of the year, and I couldn't believe how bloomin' cold it was. It was so cold I was wheezing! It's supposed to be the first day of spring tomorrow but I can't see it myself.

Nic and I are going to stay with Laura over the weekend so really looking forward to that … Tonight my car gets new tyres and a headlight check and there'll be a rush to get it through the CT tomorrow. All a last-minute rush as always! Dad will have to get up at crack of sparrows to get me to the bus in the morning. He will be well chuffed with that and he can at least come back and have a cuppa so that should keep him happy! Bet that made you smile.

Keep your fingers crossed for my car tomorrow, son, will let you know how it goes.

Take care. Stay safe. Love you loads, Mum
xxxxxxxxxxxxxxxxxxxxxxxxxxxxxxxxxxxxxxxxxxx
xxx xxxxxxxxxxxxxxxxxxxxxxxxxxxxxxxxxxxxxxxx
xxxxxxxxxxxxxxxxxxxxxxxxxxxxxxxxxxxxxxxxxxx
xxxxxxxxxxxxxxxxxxxxxxxxxxxxxxxxxxxxxxxxxxx
xxxxxxxxxxxxxxxxxxxxxxxxxxxxxx

I carried on writing … it's what I did. Then I got them all back – unopened.

Chapter 11

In the line of duty

Tuesday 1 March 2011

While out on patrol with No 2 Company, 1st Battalion Irish Guards, Lance Corporal Liam Tasker and his arms and explosives search dog, Theo, of the Royal Army Veterinary Corps 1st Military Working Dog Unit, were killed in action in the Shingazi area of Nahr-el-Sarraj in Helmand Province – known as the 'shark's fin'. Liam and Theo were sent in following the death of several troops due to IEDs in the area. Major Alex Turner, from 2 Company the Irish Guards, was told he was being sent the best, and he said: 'Liam and Theo were extremely brave and enthusiastic for the task and gave us the opportunity to be more aggressive.'

At 8.30am Liam, with Theo attached to a line at his waist, was guiding a patrol through Shingazi, an area notorious for IEDs. The mission, to reach a meeting (a *shura*) with the local Afghans and US troops, had been meticulously planned and was made possible by the confidence and assurance that came with the presence of a sniffer dog. Theo detected a threat – a plastic bag with a black wire attached – early in the mission, which bolstered the troops' morale as they moved forward, all the time edging around and through the bomb threat.

Suddenly, a 10-second burst of machine-gun fire struck the group. 'Man down. Man down! Medic!' screamed one of the Guardsmen as his colleagues returned fire and moved towards Liam, who was lying lifeless on the ground, a wound above his mouth.

The efforts of the doctor were swift and valiant, but it appeared death had been instant. There was no sign of life as Liam was lifted into a waiting vehicle and rushed to a US medical helicopter heading for Camp Bastion. Theo had been cut free of Liam and returned to Irish Guards' Kharnikah base to recuperate, but by the evening he had started fitting and was put aboard a helicopter bound for Camp Bastion. Despite the best of veterinary attention, Theo later suffered a fatal seizure. Some say Theo died of a broken heart.

Despite all attempts to save them both, Liam and his faithful war dog, Theo, died, as they had served, with courage in the line of duty.

1 March 2011
I didn't want a stranger to tell me that my son was dead.

I had told Liam that, and I remember him shrugging it off, saying, 'Shut up, Mum. Stop talking about such things.' But I tell you now that if I had that time back I would talk about all of those things. We don't realise how vital it is to have those difficult conversations until it's too late.

That morning started like so many others.

I dropped Nicola to school as normal and Jimmy and I went off to work. When Nic called me at lunchtime to say she was finishing early I went to meet my friend, Mandy, who was at the hairdressers. It was an opportunity to meet for a coffee and a chat, as we do … just to pass the time.

This is where my memory is a little hazy but I know I went home and Nic helped me to tidy up before I was due back at work. I was a bus escort for the school children so I couldn't risk being late.

When Mandy called to say the padre was looking for me I remember saying: 'I wonder why he wants to see me?' We were both involved in the Brownies so my first thought was that it could be to do with that but it still seemed a bit odd so we chatted for about half an hour about all the possibilities and then I called the padre.

'Hi, Padre. I believe you're looking for me?'

'Yes, where are you, Jane?'

'I'm at home.'

When he said he was coming to see me in 20 minutes I know I told him that it wasn't convenient. People ask me if it clicked why he was so insistent and I've always said no, but perhaps, somewhere in my head, I knew but I didn't want to be told.

I texted Mandy and told her the padre was coming to the house and she made her usual joke about getting the scones in the oven. For the first time the old scone banter wasn't funny. If I'm honest I was getting worried about the visit and she guessed it, especially when I replied, 'Fuck the scones.' I don't remember sending that text, but she did. I didn't mean to be short with her. It was pure fear talking.

I phoned Jimmy at work and asked him to guess who was coming to visit me. I convinced him it was probably to do with Brownies but I could tell he was worried. What threw both of us was that I was on my own and we thought if it was anything serious the Army would have called Jimmy and made sure he was with me.

While this was all going on in my head, I was rushing around the house with Nic doing a mad tidy – plumping cushions and moving the wet washing that was drying in the front room and all that kind of thing. I asked Nic to take the dogs upstairs and stay with them so they wouldn't bark when the padre arrived, and all of this happened in a whirl really and without much thought. Looking back I now recall Nic, who was only 13 at the time, asking me, 'Mum, do you think anything is wrong?' I reassured her that there was nothing wrong. There couldn't be because they knew I was alone.

1.30pm

I saw a car drive past the house and immediately recognised one of the people in it. It was the padre, so I asked Nic to take the dogs into her room and then went to the front door. I don't think I was totally with it, or maybe I was just in some extreme sense of denial. It's such a strange thing to explain because I think deep down I knew something was wrong. Washing hidden, dogs away … I answered the door.

'Hi, Padre. How's you?' I said, ignoring the man in front of him. I had never seen him before so I know I ignored him. Being on a military camp I was used to seeing different people, but this time I had an immediate feeling that I wasn't going to like anything he had to say.

Right then, everything started to blur.

There was a long, awkward pause and I tried to catch the padre's eye to read what was going on. Then it hit me – bang! Like a sledgehammer in the stomach. 'It's Liam, isn't it?' The other man was now in front of the padre and so suddenly right in front of me. 'How bad is he? Is it his legs? What's happened? How bad is he?' I kept asking and he kept repeating: 'Mrs Duffy, you need to listen to me. We've received some important information. Liam was killed in action earlier today …'

That's it. He had said exactly what I didn't want to hear. But I still didn't believe it. Was he sure it was Liam? How bad is it? Over and over. We were talking in circles and, to me, the man just kept shouting at me and telling me the one thing I never, ever wanted to hear. I screamed: 'My daughter! My daughter ...' Nic was upstairs and I didn't want her to see me like this. I remember the padre mis-hearing and thinking I said that I was worried about 'the dogs'. I don't think he realized that Nic was in the house.

It must have been at that point I collapsed. Nic and the padre helped me to the sofa.

How I explain to you what happened next I don't know. I felt as if I was in a nightmare, but it had to be someone else's nightmare – after all, they said that Liam was dead and that had to be wrong. Didn't it?

I needed to phone Jimmy. He was at work and the moment I spoke I sensed that he knew why I was calling. He just said: 'I'm coming home.' I couldn't wait for him to be with us as I just couldn't deal with all the questions I was being asked. They wanted my ex-husband's contact details. And this is when it became complicated – because I didn't have Ian's number.

'Mrs Duffy, do you have a number for Liam's dad?' the padre asked. 'We've been unable to reach him.'

Ian, Liam's dad, is a long-distance lorry driver so there were often times when he wasn't contactable.

And, sadly, this was one of those times. 'Ian and I have been divorced a long time. The kids are old enough to contact him themselves so I don't have a number, but I will be the one to reach him now. He needs to hear this from me, no one else. God, he will be devastated.' This really was not happening. Liam could not be dead.

All I could do was ring my daughter, Laura, to see if she had her dad's number. Laura asked if everything was OK. I said yes, everything was fine, but I needed her dad's number for Jimmy's security clearing. That was of course a lie and such a hard call to make but I didn't want to tell her about Liam over the phone. I was in Belgium and there was no way I could reach Laura in Leicester or my elder son, Ian, in Milton Keynes before the press announced later that their brother had been killed.

Liam's dad was driving when I called. 'Ian, you're going to need to pull over.' Of course he knew something was wrong. He kept asking: 'Is it Liam? How bad is he?' It seemed like ages before he parked up and put me on loudspeaker. The words echoed: 'Ian, listen to me. Liam was killed in action early this morning.' Then the deathly silence. It was heartbreaking. Then the screaming. I felt for him so much but at the same time I needed him to listen to what I had to say next.

'Listen to me, Ian, this is really important. I need your help now. Ian and Laura don't know about Liam yet so you have to go to Ian's and tell him and then both of you go to Laura.' He was about two hours away from Milton Keynes but said he would go right away to Ian's. I just wanted someone there when they found out.

I knew Laura would be wondering what on earth was going on, especially as I had asked for her dad's number. It was an odd request to make out of the blue. When the phone rang my heart sank. It was Laura and she was very upset. She asked me straight: 'What's going on, Mum? It's Liam, isn't it?' I realised from what she said that her dad was still on the road but it transpired that she had received a text from 'wee Ian's' partner, Cat, offering help if she needed it. It was all well intentioned and protective – exactly how we are as a family, but Laura had no idea what she was talking about.

This is exactly what I didn't want – to tell Laura on the phone. Even if she had guessed it was to do with Liam, this was not the way to tell her. Horror of horrors, as Laura was talking we got cut off. I screamed at the bloody phone. But maybe it was a blessing in disguise because as I was cursing and railing it turned out that her dad and her brother arrived at her door.

I wanted to tell Laura I was sorry about the communication problem and ask her to look after her dad and look after each other. My next job was to tell the rest of the family and I was well aware that we were up against time and the power of the media.

* * *

We needed to be together as a family to weather this storm so while Ian made plans to travel to our home in Belgium with Ian and Laura I started to make some calls. I tried my mum back in the UK but I couldn't reach her so I had to ask my brother Billy and my sister-in-law Lynne to track her down and tell her. The last thing I wanted was for her to hear that she had lost her grandson from anyone outside the family – or worse still from the television.

Laura had asked me: 'Mum, how's Nic? Was she with you when you were told? She will be devastated.' I think Nic must have been in shock. She was there with me the whole time, hearing the conversations, seeing me in such a mess – everything – and she still found the strength to help me when she must have been crying inside. It was Laura who said, 'My God, Mum, what are we going to do without him?' I had no answer for that. All the time in my head the words kept running: Oh God, this isn't happening. Please God, tell me this isn't happening. It's like an out-of-body experience, as if you are watching and hearing yourself from above somehow. But at the same time you are disconnected from it, as if you were watching a play based on your life and you recognise all the characters but you can't control what they say or do. I wanted to walk away but I knew I couldn't. Not from this.

The next few hours were a stream of phone calls and tears. I just wanted to get through the list and make sure everyone knew as soon as possible. I suppose in some ways it was very businesslike, but the tears weren't far away. Not for a second. Everything was happening around me but I didn't feel it was actually happening to me. I was so glad my best friends came to stay with me that first night. They helped to cushion and comfort me until Laura, Ian and Ian arrived in the early hours. I felt so lost.

At that time we didn't know that Theo had died too, only that Liam had been shot. That news came to us later in the day when the padre came over to say he had more news. When I heard that, I thought he was probably coming to say it was all a big mistake and Liam was fine. But that wasn't it at all. He said Theo had died of an unexplained seizure just hours after Liam. My first thought was at least they were together now.

Later of course we were told more about the operation and how Liam and Theo were together when their patrol came under fire. Liam fell instantly. I was told the Irish Guards did everything they could and even risked their own lives by breaking cover fire to reach Liam. They suffered serious casualties, too. The doctor tried everything at the scene and was, they said, in tears of frustration as he could not save my son. Theo, who was by his side, was rushed back to base but when his condition deteriorated the decision was made to airlift him out to Bastion for emergency care. He was fitting during the flight and then again later. Poor Theo had fought his last battle, too.

Now I'm not a vet and I know there will be Latin names for everything that happened to Theo, but in my mind Theo died of a broken heart. He saw Liam go down and he couldn't go on without him. I hope you will excuse that version of events but I have to believe that. I have to. Liam's dad said he 'truly believed that when Liam was shot Theo knew that he didn't have the person he needed there to calm him down … and his heart broke'. I think the same. They simply could not survive without each other. Now if that isn't love, I don't know what is.

When the BBC news came on the television that night it felt as if my heart stopped.

There, on the screen, was the photograph that I had been asked for just hours ago – it was Liam's favourite of himself and Theo: the two of them in the Afghan desert, the dog playfully looking over towards his master. And there were others from the media story in February showing the pair alert and ready to do their job. Theo, the 'front man', and Liam at his side. Everyone said they were a double act in every way, and maybe, in some ways, two sides of the same coin. Wherever Liam went, Theo was bound to be there walking with him or lying with him in his cot. They were inseparable and there they were on the TV, casualties of war, with a voice saying, 'The Ministry of Defence has released the name of the latest British soldier to die in Afghanistan. Lance Corporal Liam Tasker, a dog handler with the Royal Army Veterinary Corps, was killed on Tuesday while on patrol in Helmand Province. His arms and explosives search dog, Theo, died later from a seizure ... Lance Corporal Tasker, who was 26 years old, and 22-month-old Theo had completed five months of their first tour of Afghanistan. Lance Corporal Tasker's death brings to 358 the number of British military personnel to have died since the conflict began in 2001 ...'

It was true after all. I can't begin to explain what that was like. We had to switch the television off in the end. It was just too much to bear.

The media were thirsty for more on the story, especially as the loss of Theo heightened the interest in it. We didn't want the attention and I couldn't deal with it so it was best we stayed in Belgium until the media frenzy had subsided. The press didn't know we were there so we were able to lie low and come to terms with everything together before facing the music in the UK. Besides, being together meant we could help each other and the Army could help us as a unit, too. It was a terrible time. We felt almost hunted down. I didn't want to answer the phone or the door and it was hard because friends of the family wanted to call and pass on their sympathy. I hoped they understood we just couldn't deal with it.

Things happen very quickly in the military when there is a death in their 'family'. There's a procedure of care and protection and, on a more practical level, there's a procedure for handling the fallen, too. It is where the Forces are at their best. You go with the programme as it's meant to cocoon you from the outside world and reassure you that your loss has not been in vain. Nothing like this had happened on our base in Belgium before so it was a shock for everyone and it was the next day before we were allocated a liaison officer. Phil was amazing. When he arrived the day after we had our dreadful news he found us sleepless, distraught and desperate to know more about Liam's last moments. We were asking him all kinds of questions that, I realise now, he could not possibly answer at the time. Phil was alongside us 24/7. I've no idea how we would have made it through those first few days without him.

All of this is something you hear about on the television news or in the newspapers but you never think it's going to happen to you. My son had only a few weeks left of a six-month tour of duty and I still kept hoping someone would come and tell me they'd made a mistake and that Liam and Theo were alive and well after all. Later that morning, when RAVC Warrant Officer Sean Jones came over from the base in

Sennelager in Germany, I realised that this man was offering us help because I had lost my son. My son, his fellow dog soldier, had been killed in action.

So it was true and all I wanted to know at this point was – when I would get my boy home and when I'd get to see him?

Being a Forces' family you would have thought we would have known what was going to happen next, but we didn't. The problem was I was still on another planet, still crying and didn't think I would stop. At the same time, no matter how unbelievable it all was, I knew I had to get things done. It had to be right for Liam.

Chapter 12

Not again?

Liam's ZAP number came in to the communications room and the OC, Major Caroline Emmett (Officer Commanding Theatre Military Working Dog Squadron, Camp Bastion) and Sergeant Major Adrian Davies got the message fifteen minutes later and went down to wait for the helicopter with Liam on board. Adrian Davies went to Liam's room to find his passport so all the paperwork could be gathered to start the admin ball rolling. The Operation was ongoing, so, as the helicopter came in an ambulance drove onto the pad to accept Liam as a casualty. It didn't take the doctor long to announce: 'I'm sorry. He didn't make it.' It was Adrian Davies's job to identify Liam's body. 'It was all very surreal. It didn't seem long before that moment that I had seen Liam and Theo enjoying some quality time together. Liam throwing that familiar yellow ball for Theo and teasing the dog as he would one of his mates. Suddenly he was in front of me and that picture is always going to be the one that sticks in my mind. No matter what I've seen since or what I will see in the future I will not forget that. My heart went out to his family.'

The communications shutdown was still in place when Liam's death was announced to the RAVC dog team. Liam's friend and colleague, Ryan Earnshaw, was at Bastion when the OC called them together for the announcement. 'It all happened so fast. It was mental. We were crammed into the Rest Room with the OC and the padre was there so we knew it wasn't going to be good news. It was like a pressure cooker in there. I could hardly bear it. When the OC said that Liam had been killed her voice was shaking. I broke down. The lad next to me said he was sorry but he had to go. After the padre had said a few words I had to go, too. First I thought I would go to sit with Theo but then I discovered that he hadn't come back into Bastion.

'We didn't know about poor Theo then – that bad news came later. So I went to sit with Molly and shared my thoughts with her. It's something we dog handlers can do at times like that and it makes me feel sorry for the infantry guys who don't have a dog on hand to confide in. We're lucky really. I sat with Molly and cried. She didn't mind. Dogs never mind that kind of thing and she wasn't going to tell anyone. With BLT gone Molly was probably the only mate I felt comfortable being with when the old emotions kicked in.

'After that I headed for the smoking area where everyone had gathered to talk, even if they didn't smoke, and we all looked a bit shell-shocked with disbelief. I really wasn't thinking straight at all when Sergeant Major Davies came over to me and asked me if I was OK. He gave me some good advice. He told me to think about all I could do for my dog Molly and to tell her what I was going to do. He said, "Now flip it and think … if Liam hadn't died, what would he do now?" I knew what he would have done. He'd have said, "Fuck this, I'm going out," and he would have gone straight to see his dog. So that's what I did. I went back to the kennels.

'An hour later I was due to go out on patrol with a colleague but it wasn't our call sign so we headed back to base where we saw a cluster of soldiers with the OC. It was the guys from the Irish Guards. Their Major Turner gave an incredibly emotional speech. It was very stirring and filled me with great strength. He said to his men: "You've heard today that Liam has been killed so you all keep an eye on them – he pointed to me and my mate. We're going back out and we're going to poke the enemy."

For those who had been at Bastion when Ken Rowe and Sasha were killed in action three years earlier the news was difficult to absorb. Chris Ham, now Lieutenant Colonel, heard the news from Camp

Bastion and took it like a body blow. 'To have this happen a second time to one of our own was devastating news. Afghanistan was the biggest anti-terrorist project we, as dog handlers, had faced since Northern Ireland. By 2011 half the soldiers killed in Helmand were the victims of roadside bombs and the threat was growing, which meant a massive demand on the search dogs and handlers. We sent as many as we could to service the wider Army even though we knew the demand was always going to outweigh our resources. We trained them and sent them because the dogs, ultimately, saved lives out there. It's as simple as that.

'Liam Tasker had a very close bond with Theo and they worked as a close and effective team for the five months they had together. Liam was a good soldier, not only a handler, and Theo was an exceptional search dog. Together they were an effective team and both man and dog would be greatly missed by anyone who had met either of them or served with them. They did their job on the front line of battle, and saved many lives. Ken Rowe and Liam Tasker faced an enemy who shows no mercy and who believes life is cheap, a terrorist force that will not give up or give in and whose ever-advancing acts of terror know no bounds. These young soldiers and their dogs did all we asked of them. They used their training to do the job they loved at the highest level. They died in the pursuit of evil while protecting their fellow soldiers. No one could ask more of any soldier or dog.'

It was late afternoon on 1 March when Liam's best mate, Karl Ingram, was on the way back from a training session with 101 MWD Regiment in North Luffenham. The new OC wanted everyone back in for a briefing. 'Something was wrong and my gut was telling me it was Liam or another operator on tour. I couldn't wait for the briefing to find out so I called a mate at the DAC to see if he had been told anything. He couldn't say but called me back a few minutes later. There it was, the dreaded news: "Karl, it's Liam. Liam's dead."

'I remember the sheer life of me empty. Not being able to control my emotions I left the room and broke down away from prying eyes. I've never felt as empty and inconsolable as I did that moment. My thoughts ran wild with visions of my previous tours and I tried to piece together what might have happened to Liam and it was torturing me. Then my thoughts switched to his family and to Leah, his girlfriend. I knew they would be absolutely distraught and I felt I had to try to understand what could have happened to him. But then we go out front – dog and handler – we go ahead of the troops. Stepping into unknown territory.'

Karl had known Liam a long time and even though they didn't hit it off at first they shared a passion for sport that soon brought them together. 'Liam was surprisingly agile in the ropes as I found out, and with the boxing and the celebrating in the bar after we soon became mates. When we were both posted to the DAC on a course we became virtually inseparable. We drank, partied, drank some more and terrorised the block with our terrible DJ'ing and our dreams of becoming superstar DJs.

'We spoke about everything, defended each other, cared and looked after each other. I have never had and will never have a friend like him again.

'My Staff Sergeant, Tack Thompson, was brilliant with me in those moments, and so was my friend Haydon. I will never forget their compassion. As soon as I got myself together I went to see my OC and requested to be at Liam's repat. I didn't want strangers carrying him onto home soil.'

Just hours after the announcement of Liam's death the RAVC released the news that the unit had lost one more of its own – their dog, Theo. Despite all efforts by the Irish Guards to lift Theo clear of the attack and airlift him back to Bastion for emergency care, the impact of the firefight had proved too much for the young dog with so much life and loyalty still to give. As with Sasha before him, Theo's body was cremated and his ashes stored in a specially polished and engraved shell casing for the sombre repatriation to the UK. He, too, would make the journey home beside his master.

* * *

The death of Ken Rowe still cast a shadow over the unit. Liam had met Ken; it was when they reached their Class 2. Ken was with his friend Lance Corporal Ian 'Russ' Russell when he asked Russ, 'Who's that?' It turned out to be Liam, who was off duty and out with his mates playing the 'Steve Parry' game – shouting 'Are you Steve Parry?' to random people in the street! It made him and the others laugh. They both liked a joke, they shared the same love of dogs, and the same drive and passion for the job.

Both were also fiercely devoted to their families and proud that they had the best families in the world. Ken, Newcastle born and bred and pure Geordie – who would drink Newcastle Brown Ale even though he didn't like it – and Liam the Scot, born in Fife, who left his heart in his homeland but believed in living the dream wherever life took him. The job they shared sped them down different paths but they had one massive thing in common: they were dog soldiers to the core. To lose Liam was, for some, like losing Ken all over again.

'Everyone was crying, from the OC down the ranks,' recalls Ryan. 'We had lost two more of our own. It doesn't get any worse than that. We were in a state of disbelief, but fortunately when you're in a war zone the Army doesn't give you much time for self-pity and introspection, and with the repatriation process already in motion it was good to be able to channel our feelings into giving Liam and Theo a good send-off.

'Sadly, repatriations were by then a familiar sight at Bastion. It didn't make them less meaningful, just a dreaded part of the Camp routine. As a unit we were luckier than most because our losses were not as great as others, but it was different for the infantry guys. They were sometimes losing more than one a day and soon didn't need to rehearse their repats. We decided we wanted to do a vigil for Liam and Theo which, because it involved all the dogs and handlers, was a bit more of a personal goodbye from his mates. The CO of the Irish Guards was a good bloke and he gave the OK for us to keep two dogs back for the vigil and I promised to cover the ground with Molly the next day.

'I sorted everyone around the parade ground and then I wondered if the dogs would be OK hearing the bugle. Molly was fine but my mate's dog, Jack, howled the whole time. It was a totally surreal moment and Liam would have loved it. He would have cried with laughter!

'Poor Jack and Duffy, his handler, sat it out while I led the vigil with Molly. We marched from the parade ground back to the kennels and arrived just in time to go out on patrol with the Irish Guards. We still had a job to do and Liam would have wanted us to get out there with the lads anyway.'

The bearer party was assembled and rehearsals fitted in to the normal daily routine. Ryan Earnshaw put himself up for the job but the death of Lance Corporal Stephen McKee of the Irish Guards meant Ryan was pulled back to cover ground. Lance Corporal McKee was on a strike out when the vehicle he was travelling in hit a roadside IED. It was another sign that dogs were needed out there and needed more than ever.

While arrangements were made to get Karl Ingram to RAF Lyneham to take part in the repatriation of Liam's body to the UK, his colleagues in Afghanistan were preparing to honour their mate in the heat and the dirt of a war zone. Sergeant Matt Jones made ready to lead the bearer party: 'It's a hard fact but there's no time to grieve properly when you're out in theatre but we all felt the loss. Liam was a big personality and he left a big gap for many of us. He was missed by his mates and by every battle group he had supported in the five months he had served in Afghan. The best we could do for our mate was to see him off well and with the honour he deserved. Once that plane left our sky we needed to have the peace of mind that he was going home and we had done our best.

'Those of us left behind had to hold our hurt back. Back home I knew my wife and daughter would be rocked by the news of Liam's death. They would see it on the news and worry. The thing is it brings you face to face with your own mortality, but you have to carry on.'

All eyes looked upwards as the C17 slipped down from the sky and landed, kicking up dust and debris in its wake. What was particularly poignant about this repat was that the incoming plane was carrying the squadron due to replace Liam's. He was only two weeks off going home.

'Repats are hard on everyone and there's something about the fact that they take place in the middle of the night that really gets to you,' recalls Sergeant Major Davies. 'The C17 comes into Bastion and we all hear it for a good while before its huge shadow comes into view.

'The turnout for the repat was the very best we could put together for Liam and Theo at a time when the troops were being hit so hard 24/7. They had their own losses to deal with but I know they felt the loss of Liam and Theo as much as we did. A lot of the guys had said that apart from the reassurance of seeing a search dog upfront on patrol there was a feeling of normality and domesticity seeing a spaniel running around and sniffing in the dirt during down time at Bastion. All handlers had a bit of an ongoing battle with some of the lads who like to fuss and feed the dogs, so we were always reminding them that they were military WORKING dogs – full stop. But we could all see how our four-legged soldiers were a great comfort out there, and somehow, as dogs do, they always sensed when they were needed for that special job. We never held them back from going where they were needed. Why would we?

'Repatriation is the hardest duty I've ever had to perform as a soldier. I didn't want to break down in front of the troops but I'd be lying if I said I wasn't close. It was tough, really tough putting Liam and Theo in the back of that C17. That was it – the end of it all.'

Chapter 13

Repatriation: the final journey home

JANE

I can tell you right away that nothing, absolutely nothing, can prepare you for the emotional overload that hits you on the day you go to meet the plane carrying your son's body home. The Army is beside you. They guide you and protect you from the press and anything or anyone that intends to trespass upon your grief bubble. It's then I realised that the Army was my extended family, too, not just my son's, and they don't want to see any more hurt descend on any of us. Everyone from the welfare officer assigned to the family through to Liam's friends, colleagues and commanding officers tries to prepare you, at least for the practicalities involved – the who, what and when of it all – but, believe me, there is nothing, no amount of planning or consideration, that can reduce the massive impact of that day.

Remember, we had gone from organising our leave to coincide with Liam's return from Afghan at the end of March and suddenly we were having to prepare for his funeral. There are no words to describe how I was feeling. I know that on 1 March 2011 a part of me died inside and it's true that I will never be the same again. Yes. I go about my day-to-day life because I have to for my other children but there have been many times when I've thought about just going to be with Liam. I know how that sounds and I appreciate that not everyone will understand that but I've always brought myself back from the brink. After all – how could I do that to my family when they are grieving too?

After the words 'killed in action' we started to hear the word 'repatriation'. I remember thinking, 'What the hell is repatriation?' Phil explained that Liam was to be repatriated back into the UK on 9 March and, for me, that really meant that I was finally getting my boy home. But that was just the start of it. We had no idea of exactly what was ahead of us.

We stayed in Belgium for a week to avoid the glare of the media. The SHAPE (Supreme Headquarters Allied Powers Europe) base is a community all of its own and everyone there really looked after us. They even gave us a reason to leave our house for the first time in four days when, on 4 March, they renamed their annual Tri-Star Challenge fundraising event to become the Tri-Service Challenge for the Liam Tasker Trophy. Involving competitors from the Navy, Army and RAF, as well as the NATO civilians on the base, the sporting challenge raises money for charity (mainly Help 4 Heroes). We were honoured by their tribute to Liam and honoured to attend. As we now do every year.

We were still on a military camp and very protected from the outside world, but the outside world was waiting for us when we got home to Tayport in Scotland. The news of Liam's death was still attracting media interest and the Ministry of Defence press office had dealt with the military side of things but I suppose that wasn't enough for them. The news of Theo's death just added to the intense sense of loss and I can understand that, but it's still hard to be in the middle of it all. I think the most difficult thing, for all of us, was that we had already been looking forward to Liam coming home.

He had chatted over the details with Leah on the Sunday before he was killed so we were expecting him home on 27 March and making plans to meet him from RAF Brize Norton and bring him home. By Tuesday those plans had changed beyond hope. Liam was coming home to us but the last thing we expected was that it would be the repatriation of his body.

Life for my family in Scotland had been turned upside down, too. Liam's grandmother (my mother) was in pieces and I knew that anything I said would never be enough to heal her. We soon ran out of words and just cried together. Liam had been very close to his grandma Janette and she was so proud of him joining the Army. It was like seeing my brother, Richard, go through it all again. Watching him grow up from a boy to a soldier so happy and so proud to be doing the job he loved. Her home was like a shrine to Richard and his Army career – photos everywhere. And I was going the same way with Liam – everything he did, and there it was captured in a photograph. Funny to think that the collection was now sadly complete.

Ian had headed back to the UK with Ian and Laura after the Tri-Star Challenge and had started to prepare for the repatriation. My brother Rich and his wife, Lynne, were a tower of strength. As an Army officer Rich knew what to do about things and that was such a weight lifted off my shoulders and a much-needed layer of protection at a time I was feeling so confused and vulnerable.

I was dreading the journey to RAF Lyneham but at least we didn't have to go under our own steam. The military sent a car for all of us which took the pressure off a little because I know I couldn't have driven all those miles feeling the way I did and I knew that Jimmy was not up to it either. He was feeling the strain, too. I know he felt helpless being unable to stop the grief. I think it's hard on the menfolk because there's so much they feel they have to hold back. They feel they have to be the strong ones but they are still feeling the same as us inside. I'm glad Jimmy was holding it together, though, as I think I needed him to comfort the girls and Leah, Liam's girlfriend, too, while I sorted myself out. It was a very strange feeling. It was happening: there we all were, my son and my husband in dark suits, me and the girls in our black. We were going to see Liam home but no one was laughing or sharing stories about him. Nothing was normal.

That was the most telling sign of all. Usually we would be talking about Liam all the time. Remembering his jokes and making sure we had all his favourite beer and food in ready for him. It was like Christmas every time, and I loved it. And I know he looked forward to coming home and all the home comforts, too. He would always joke with me for getting too much food and booze but then say: '... but then I am your favourite, your golden child, so that's all good, Mother!'

I wished so much that we were all going to Brize to meet him and bring him home on leave – tour of duty completed. But we weren't. I knew that we were going to RAF Lyneham to meet his coffin and I really wasn't sure I could bear it.

BRINGING LIAM HOME

After hearing the news of his friend's death Karl Ingram was sent home for a long weekend ahead of the repatriation. Karl was ready for the practical preparations for his role as bearer but emotionally he was still caught in a state of disbelief. 'When you find yourself in this awful situation you realise that apart from being there for your mate you have actually been given the greatest honour – to bear one of our fallen heroes. The ceremony is steeped in tradition and comes with so many responsibilities, the best and worst of all being a responsibility to his mother and father. There's no getting away from the reality that you are carrying their son and you know the first glimpse of his coffin is going to hit them so bloody hard.

'When I returned to work on the Monday before the repat I discovered that my Staff Sergeant, Tack Thompson, had arranged for a Colour Sergeant from the Irish Guards to come over and help me and the lad who'd be mirroring me (Matty Way) to run through what would be expected of us and organise some practice. The practical instruction was really appreciated; after all, it was a first for most of us. But for me, the best advice he shared in the days leading up to the "big one" came in one sentence. I remember him saying: "Boys, our friend is no longer here; this is not how we will remember him, this is just weight." At the time I wasn't sure if that would help me, but later on I know that it did.

'When the big day arrived the seven-strong bearer party came together at RAF Lyneham and although it was a morbid affair it was great to see so many faces who all cared about the big man. We said a few words, shook hands and did the small-talk thing but, for once, where Liam was concerned, there were no jokes and no laughter throughout the coffin drill. Everything learnt on this day was professional and throughout the day our skills and drills were ironed out until we were ready to perform our duties to perfection.

'What I now recognise as the hardest day of my Army career finally arrived. I don't think I slept a great deal the night before and when I woke up I found myself going over and over my kit with a fine-toothed comb, looking to correct the smallest imperfection. I simply wasn't going to allow anything to be less than perfect. Funny thing is, I don't remember how I spent the hours leading up to the drive to the air terminal but that's probably because, whatever I was doing, my mind was already focused on what lay ahead. It was time to "suit up": my boots were buffed to the highest mirrored shine, my uniform crisply pressed and my medals shone and dazzled on my chest. We all looked immaculate. Nothing was left to chance. A wee drink was had to calm the nerves and then it was time to bring our friend home and present him, with honour, to his family.

'We lined up in formation – three men with another three parallel to each other with a seventh at the rear of the party calling out the timings. This was a safety measure in case our greatest fear came true and we stumbled coming down the ramp onto the airstrip. We awaited our command. Focused and silent we watched the C17 land and taxi in and rest. I remember my stomach churning over and over until, eventually, the command to "step off" came through. Heads held high, we marched towards the gaping black hole in the plane. I felt full of emotion, enough to burst, but at every step the overriding thought was "Please don't mess up, for God's sake don't mess up." I fixed my eyes on the man in front and that seemed to calm me enough to keep my feet moving one in front of the other.

'In reality I know it only took a few minutes to march to our designated spot but it seemed to take forever. I'm sure my brain was trying to delay the impact of what was coming next because I can tell you that walking up the ramp into the belly of the plane, out of sight of everyone else there, is not the worst of it. Nothing can compare with the horror of being faced with the sight of the Union flag draped over your friend.

'For some of us it was too much to take in at that moment and I remembered the invaluable words of the Irish Guards Colour Sergeant which had been echoing in my head. I repeated his words out loud to the group as we stood there, our task at our feet: "Boys, our friend is no longer here; this is not how we will remember him, this is just weight." I took my place and then took the weight with the others.

'I remember saying to myself, fuck, he's heavy!!! But knowing he was in full kit with all his equipment – as per the regulations – that should not have been a surprise. Feet firm but shifting slightly to rest the weight comfortably on our shoulders, we all fixed our faces and looked dead ahead. Together we stepped forward, slow pace, down the slippery off ramp – seven men bringing their friend home to rest. Back to his family. Theo was home too. The shell casing containing his ashes was resting beside Liam's coffin ready to be lifted off separately, once we had Liam safely away.

'The march was hard and I felt every single step of it in my throat. For most of the walk you remain completely inside yourself, totally focused on where you are and what you are doing. And that was OK until the moment I saw, out of the corner of my eye, Liam's family standing together holding on to each other. I could hear their devastation, pain and tears. It took everything I had to contain myself and remain focused through to the end. We marched towards the waiting hearse where we carefully placed Liam for the journey to the Chapel of Rest and on to Wootton Bassett.

'Our job was almost done and I actually felt the relief of the weight as it left my shoulders and we turned and marched off the flight pan. Thank God I managed to get out of sight before the emotion caught up with me. It hit me like a train. My nerves were shot to pieces and I couldn't contain the tears. And I wasn't alone. We all crumpled under the pressure of the emotion. Soldiers, yes, but men, too, and we remembered that the weight we just carried was our mate. I'm not sure why things happen as they do but I'm sure Liam had to be watching because after a few smokes and a few minutes to pull myself together I suddenly realised I'd done the whole parade with my fly undone! It was like Liam had played one final prank on me, and I had to laugh. He would have loved that. It was just his style. Thanks, mate!

'I stubbed out my cigarette and went back inside for the next phase of the day and a debrief from the hierarchy. As soon as that was over a steward called me over to say that Liam's mum Jane and his girlfriend Leah had asked to speak to me before proceedings continued. There wasn't much time because of the tight timings of everything, but we hugged – no words were needed this time. I'd spoken to her on the phone after she'd received Liam's final letter which I had found amongst his belongings in his room at Luffenham. She told me that he had spoken kindly of me and in the letter and that he had apologised in advance for asking me to carry his 'fat ass' – twice. In the blur of it all I don't recall what I said to her but I was glad that I had done something to help them and comfort them.

'The day did not finish there and what followed truly amazed me and still does whenever I think of it.

It started as the hearse left the gates of RAF Lyneham on its journey to Oxford via Wootton Bassett. All along the route members of the RAF Police Dog section in full uniform and their dogs created a guard of honour. One after another the men and women of the section stood, heads bowed, to honour Liam and Theo as the hearse passed by. Liam would most likely have overseen the training of many of the dogs that attended, so that was a true show of respect for the "big man".

'Members of our own squadron were there, too, and the distress was clear to see on every face. It was an incredibly sad and sombre sight, made more poignant by the hundreds – it certainly looked like hundreds – of local people standing quietly with their dogs to pay their respects to the partnership of Liam and Theo. The hearse was covered in flowers of all kinds. All through the town people of all ages were stepping out of the crowd to place them on the roof as the cortège passed slowly by.

'I'm not sure how many people attended Wootton Bassett that day but we all thought it must have been thousands. It was awesome to witness. Breathtaking, really, to see my friend honoured in such a way. And his family beside him. And I'm going to say it now – thank you, Royal Wootton Bassett, thank you. Thank you for what you did for my friend Liam and his family and for so many before and after.

'It was a truly humbling experience that I will remember always. I think I went back to Aldershot still in a daze. To be honest I think all of us did. That evening we saluted the big man with a customary glass of something – the rest is a blur. But I know that Liam would have approved.'

JANE

People kept saying to me, 'You're as brave as that Christina Schmid. So strong. A real inspiration …' I wasn't anything like that brave woman. I was a mess. It was nice of people to say that to help me along but the truth of it was that even when I wasn't crying on the outside I was hysterical on the inside. I was just not prepared at all for the repatriation. How could anyone be prepared for something like that?

It was a very grey, dull day and I couldn't help wishing for some sun. Liam would have liked that, even after five months of Afghan heat he would have preferred the sunshine to the grim conditions that met us that day. You could tell that the people who were there to help and guide us through the procedure were well practised, and we all know the sad truth about that, but it helped because I was pretty much 'not there' in my head.

We were told that Liam would be the only soldier being repatriated on that flight but I knew he would have Theo for company, which he would have wanted anyway. When I had asked about Theo's ashes I was reassured that they would be coming home with my son on the same flight and the shell casing placed beside the coffin. I had a feeling that Liam's colleagues would have wanted that anyway. The dog and the man belonged together.

They said the foggy, windy weather was going to cause a problem with visibility and offered us the opportunity to watch the plane arrive on a screen indoors. It was so odd. We all sat together in a small room staring at the tiny screen in the corner waiting and hoping for something to appear.

Laura and Nicola were clinging to me and Leah was distraught as we were all transfixed to the monitor on the wall. We couldn't see the plane but we could hear it, and I will never forget that sound. And then something flashed into sight. That was it. Our only view of the plane. We hadn't realised that it was a static CCTV camera, so not actually following the aircraft at all. I felt a surge of panic. Where was Liam? We had heard the plane land so I knew my boy was home. I wanted to see him.

The next few minutes were excruciating while we waited for the coffin to be de-flagged. We were escorted outside and shown into a large marquee where we were asked to sit down. Our view was of the massive black aircraft that I knew contained my son's body. The bearer party marched to the plane and disappeared inside for what seemed like ages, and then … they emerged bearing my son on their shoulders. There he was – there was my son. I wanted to run to him. We had been told to remain seated but all I wanted to do was get out of my chair and run to my son and hold him so close. I have never felt pain like that pain.

I felt the tears come harder and I couldn't stop them. I know I was wailing, in a state of agony. There was my son. Right in front of me, and I could not move. I just wanted to go to Liam but I was conscious of my girls sitting either side of me holding my hands. They needed me to be strong and I was doing my best to be everything for them, but then I just lost control. The crying would not stop as I watched the coffin being carried away, and I was dying inside. I watched as my son was transferred to the hearse for his short journey to the Chapel of Rest. I just couldn't move. I watched the car drive away until it had completely gone from sight.

It was then I suddenly realised that I was sitting there on my own and I think I would still be there if the lovely and very helpful RAF padre hadn't offered to help me to my feet. I couldn't walk. My legs kept crumpling underneath me. The padre was very kind and made sure that I found the rest of my family who had helped each other back to the initial reception room where we were offered refreshments ahead of our visit to the chapel.

Talk about a surreal moment. I remember the lovely lady there offering sandwiches from a huge selection she had arranged for us. They looked delicious but my children are so fussy that I ended up asking for something simple like ham or cheese instead. I was pretty embarrassed, especially as I suddenly realised the minibus was waiting for us and we wouldn't have time to eat the food after all, so, for some reason I still don't understand, I asked for all the food to be put in doggy bags to take away with us. So there I was, in a mini-bus heading for the Chapel of Rest with a huge bag of wrapped sandwiches. To this day I have no idea why I did that, unless, maybe, I hoped one of us would feel like eating again and I would have something to give them. As it turned out, no one ate a thing. No one spoke. We just cried. A lot.

I suppose it goes without saying that the Chapel of Rest was too much for all of us. Every care was taken by the military to make us feel at ease and, thank God, we had each other to lean on. Looking back at it now it was one more out-of-body experience in a growing number of similar experiences since we heard that Liam had been killed in action. But this was something I wouldn't wish on anyone, not even my worst enemy.

My kids seemed to be looking at me and I knew I had to be strong for them so I had to try to compose myself before we went through that door. It was all so surreal. We sat in a corridor waiting – me, Jimmy, Ian, Laura, Ian and Nicola – and, standing guard, a military policeman. A reminder that Liam's death was under investigation. There were candles for you to light at the end and, if my memory serves me right, it had the feel and look of a small portable cabin made to look like a chapel of rest. So sad that there had been so many families through here that it had necessitated this special place. I didn't want to be there but I was relieved that my son was home.

Everything had been prepared for us. I can't remember who went in first to see Liam but I think it was his dad, Ian. I wanted to be the last, I don't know why, but I didn't want anyone in after me. I will never forget walking into that small room with my son's coffin draped in the Union flag. I wasn't sure if I wanted to step forward or run away. Suddenly the room grew smaller and I was at his side. Desperate to see him, but at the same time wanting to look away, I fixed on the coffin – it was closed with a a brass plaque with his name on the lid. I cried. I screamed. My family tell me I was still wailing when I ran outside. I needed some time out of there and I thought I was going to be sick on the spot if I stayed. That was his coffin right in front of me. My son was in that box. My boy. My son. I didn't want my kids to see me like that so I made my excuses and went to sit in the mini-bus alone. I didn't want to leave Liam in that room but I had to. I knew that the military timings would mean we had to move on but what I didn't realise was that it would be three weeks before I would have my son home to rest in peace.

I'm sure I was hysterical. I've been told since that I was, but how else could I be? Liam's dad and brother were distraught and the girls inconsolable. We just clung to each other as if our own lives depended on it: 'I love you, son. I love you ...' was all I could say and I wanted him to know that for sure as I stood there beside him.

I didn't think about Theo right then but I had been told that his ashes had been taken from the plane and were being kept for me to have later. I understood the need for the focus to be on the fallen soldier, not the soldier dog; and besides, I knew, without a shadow of a doubt, that Liam's friends would be looking after Theo and would want to say their private goodbyes to him too. It was their time with him now: we would have ours later. Just knowing he was home was enough for me.

I realise now that there are days in your life when no matter how hard you try to stay in control and be everything to everyone it all goes to pieces; 9 March 2011 was one of those days. I'm not sure what my family and friends expected of me but I hope I didn't fall too short. There must have been moments when I gave the impression that I was on top of the situation, stoic and all that. But somewhere along the line I lost it.

We had flowers. We all had flowers to put on the hearse. Red roses and carnations were everywhere. People of all ages were there, even small children waiting to present their flowers. I would have cried over that if I had not been crying already. At the start of this horror story I wasn't sure I could handle the stop in Wootton Bassett. My first thought was that I didn't want to share my son with strangers. But when it was explained to me that the hearse would pause so people could pay their respects I realised that my son deserved that and so I decided to go ahead. I've never regretted it.

The number of RAVC and RAF Police dogs and handlers lining the route, from the moment we left the gates of RAF Lyneham, was incredible. They bowed their heads as we passed. I was in pieces. As we reached Wootton Bassett we were met by the crowds of people lining the street. Reporters and photographers were everywhere; they were even standing on the rooftops. We had been prepared for the high media presence but it was still astounding to see just how many people had taken the trouble to be there. Civilians had brought their dogs along to stand in silence beside the military dogs. The mix of the military and non-military was immensely touching. When I look back I still find it hard to believe that all happened. It was so surreal.

I'm sure Liam would have been able to name the dogs there that he had trained – and it would have been a fair few. I know that because that was his job, and his dream job, too. It was what he wanted to pick up again when he got back from Afghan. He loved that job so damn much, which is probably why he was such a task-master. He told me he used to say to the trainees: 'If you're here to be dog handler you'd best do it properly!' He believed in doing a job well or don't do it at all and I admired and respected him for that.

The funeral bell tolled as the car dropped us at the designated spot and the crowd gathered us in as if we were being hugged. The huge emotional silence was eerie. I'm sure people spoke to me but the drone of the bell was really all I could hear above the sound of the sobbing in my head. We stood side by side, me, the girls, Leah and the boys, as the hearse drew to a halt. The line of military standards held by British Legion veterans lowered in sequence, their tips covered in black velvet. The man in undertakers' garb leading the cortège turned to face the coffin, removed his tall hat and bowed his head. Then the crowd started to move person by person towards the hearse. The flowers were coming from all directions. A boy of about five or six years old was lifted up to put his flowers on top of the hearse. It was so touching and I knew Liam would have approved, especially if the little one's tribute was for Theo too.

We stepped forward to give Liam the flowers we had been holding so tightly, but seeing the coffin again was already too much for me. I wanted to hold him but the best I could do was put the palm of my hand up to the window of the hearse and say: 'I love you, son …' I'm sure I didn't say it out loud but a journalist must have lip-read what I said and the next day the papers carried the quote.

Chapter 14

I really miss you, son ...

I'm really not sure how we all made it through Liam's repatriation, but we did – just about. They say there are several stages to the grieving process and I'm not sure where we all were after the repatriation. I was still feeling a huge sense of loss confused with not really believing that it had happened. Sometimes I would think it was all a bad dream and Liam would suddenly appear large as life, wondering what all the glum faces were about, and give me a big hug. But then reality hit and the tears would come back with force. There really is no way of escaping the truth.

I was still haunted by the scene of the hearse driving away out of Wootton Bassett. To me, they were driving Liam away from me, and at the time I didn't know where he was going. I later found out that he was being taken to the John Radcliffe Hospital in Oxford for the autopsy. I don't think it would have helped to know that at the time. Not at all. For all of our emotional turmoil there was the military process too. The autopsy and inquest lay ahead, but for me the day was a weird slice of someone else's life. Another mother who had lost her son. Not me. Until the tears returned.

I can't deny that there were members of the family who reached the anger stage ahead of me. They were concerned that the huge attention Liam and Theo were given in the media two weeks before they died had made them a Taliban target. They were wondering – should we have tried to get him home earlier? They said if we had requested it he would have been sent home alive and none of this would have happened. Had we let our boy down?

If Liam had been around to ask I know what he would have said. Liam's answer would have been 'no', we had not let him down. I know my son and he would have been furious with us. He was a young man who loved his job and was proud of his achievements. To ask for him to be pulled out just ahead of his tour ending would have made it worse. He was already dreading leaving Theo to carry on working without him. Besides, he was restless when he was home. The job was his life. He wanted to be out there with his mates and protecting the lads with Theo at his side.

When the Army filmed Liam and Theo going through their paces at Camp Bastion just two weeks before they died the world saw, in a way they maybe hadn't before, just how skilled and valuable dogs like Theo are in the military. They are with the troops on the front line, working in the face of danger, which is why the dogs are so well loved and respected. It's why Liam was proud to be the soldier chosen for the job and why he would have died with honour doing the job he loved and for his country. If God had granted it, Liam would have made it his life's work.

Was I angry? Yes, I was angry, angry with God, for a wee while at least. But I've always believed so I decided to reach an agreement with Him. He already had my dad and now Liam was with Him, too, so I asked Him to look after them both until it was my turn. I reached my decision and made my peace with God so I left my disappointment in Him behind. If ever I needed my faith it was then, and besides, what does anger get you? Nothing, and it was never going to bring Liam back to me, and that's all I wanted.

Part of the torture of losing a loved one who dies serving overseas is that no sooner are you over one thing than you are preparing for the next. It's painful, like a long drawn-out goodbye. Liam's funeral was going to be the last step and the biggest for all of us to bear. I can honestly say that I never expected to have to organise a funeral for one of my children.

I kept asking when would Liam be home as I was desperate to hold his funeral before 26 March, which was Nicola's birthday. It was her 14th birthday that year, bless her. She had shared so much with me and I didn't want her special day to be overshadowed, as it would have been. That was inevitable. She deserved more and Liam wouldn't have wanted me to put anything before Nic's happiness that day.

Liam came home to Scotland on 17 March. His funeral was five days later.

He would be laid to rest at home in Tayport with full military honours. The service took place in the church where he was christened and the place my family call home. In the military, because you move about so much, you have to have a spiritual home, somewhere everything and everyone comes back to at the end of everything. I also wanted to make sure that Liam's last wishes were carried out just as he had set down in his final letter to me. That was so important to me, and no one was going to stand in my way.

It was typical of Liam to make his last letter to me something I could re-read and laugh and cry all at the same time. He called it his 'admin', which in Forces' language is all part of the paperwork that has to be completed before a tour of duty. Insurance, a final will and testament and last letters to loved ones … just in case. I can imagine Liam putting pen to paper and thinking, never going to need this but here we go. It will keep my mother happy.

Four days after hearing of Liam's death we were told that Liam's final letter to his family had been found and it was ready to be handed over. I wasn't aware of this right away as Phil, our liaison officer, contacted my brother Rich and they met so the letter could be handed into our care discreetly and privately. Maybe Phil felt it would be better coming to me from Rich than anyone outside the family. He obviously knew how upset I would be and Rich would be able to pick the right moment. It turned out there were messages for all of us and, although I was relieved that Liam had left something, to actually sit down to read through it all was quite a different matter.

Rich was the perfect person to hand the letters to me. I wasn't home at the time but when he gently told me he had something for me I skipped the shopping and headed back. I took the envelope from him and held it tight. I can't tell you what I was thinking but I remember taking a good deep breath before Jimmy and I went into the bedroom to read it together. I want to share the letter he wrote to me. I never thought I could do that but I'm ready. All I ask is that you please remember that he was a young lad writing this to his family – just in case he was killed in action. That's the massive tragedy of it all: he wrote it thinking it would never be read.

In a weird way I was happy, happy that his letter included something for everyone and, when it came to his funeral arrangements, he knew what he wanted. Liam was only 26 years old, with his whole life ahead of him: a job he loved and a girlfriend he adored – life was sweet. The thought of him sitting down to write a 'final' letter still haunts me but it also makes me smile. Liam didn't write letters – I was the one who wrote the letters – and there he was writing the most important letter of his life.

I took that deep breath:

Hi ya Mum
Wow!! Where do I start? ... Obviously if you read this then the worst has happened (well this is weird lol) but I don't want anyone to feel down or wonder if things could've been different if ... What's meant to be is meant to be!! I want everyone to get drunk and try to move on with their lives. One thing I do want to say though is that I've had a fantastic life, I've got the best family in the world – you're all amazing despite your own little flaws. I look and listen to all the people I've met moan and groan about their families all the time and I cannot comment. I've had an amazing upbringing and I thank you all for that!! ... Mum you mean the absolute world to me and I know this sounds like a bit of a cliché (if that's how you spell it!!) but I honestly cannot find the words to describe what you mean to me!! How you spawned me I don't know. Lol! ...
Here's something for everyone ...

Jimmy … You gave up so much to make me the man I became and I can't thank you enough.

Laura, one of my older yet younger sisters … I am so so proud of you, everything you have done and are going to achieve …

Nicola … You really are an amazing young lady and I've always said that god forbid if I ever had kids if they turned out to be half as smart, beautiful or as brave as you are I would be one lucky man.

Ian … you truly are a legend dude, always there for me despite all our arguments and fallouts in the past. I always knew you would be there to support me whatever decisions I made.

Now for the boring bit. I want everyone to get drunk and every year I want my mates to mark my death with a rugby match. And for my funeral I want you to play Metallica's 'The Day that Never Comes', 'The Funeral' by Band of Horses and 'Sailing' by Christopher Cross.

And sorry lads I want you all (he lists the names) to carry my fat ass … I figure with your combined weight you will manage it! I have a whole list of jobs for other people but I know the Army still has to function!

'Each day's a gift and not a given right.' This was going to be my next tattoo and I've tried to live my life around this ethos and I would love for you all to do the same!! I'm sorry this letter is a bit short and sweet … but I hope I've given everyone a tiny idea as to how much you lot mean to me … You will always be in my heart and I'll see you on the other side.

My love forever and always

X Liam X

'A man will walk many miles whilst chasing his dreams.'

It was heartbreaking to read. I have only read the letter three times since that day but the contents have got me through many a dark moment, I can tell you. It was just typical Liam – like having him back in the room. It is really strange but Liam seemed to know exactly what people needed to hear from him and, at times, he gave us a rare glimpse of Liam thinking hard about his future. He even talks about if he had kids – bless him. He also said how he would like to be remembered with the annual rugby match and his mates enjoying a good booze-up in his name. My God he would wish he was there with them too.

Sometimes he forgot that the letter had to be in the past tense so there are alterations all the way through, like the mention of having kids: he forgot that it should have been 'if I had had kids', and where he had realised his mistake he scribbled it out and corrected it. Liam wrote as if he was speaking to all of us in turn and although it was typically random in his thoughts it was thoughtful and he was always a thoughtful boy. Laura says that's what she misses most about Liam: whatever the situation he always said the right thing to make people feel better. She misses that most of all, and Nicola misses his sense of humour. Everything was laced with a laugh – even the last letter.

I didn't want to think about the funeral but after the repatriation it was the focus of all my days. When the Army padre came to see me I could tell that he wasn't impressed with Liam's choice of music. I think it was the mention of Metallica that made his eyes roll but he seemed a good sport and admitted: 'I've never done anything like that before but I'm sure there won't be a problem.' The RAVC slow march (Golden Spurs) had to be played on entering the church but at the close of the service and as the congregation left I requested (probably demanded) we play the Metallica and Christopher Cross tracks Liam wanted. It was important to me that Liam got to hear the music he had chosen and to know that his final wishes had been carried out.

I wanted to make sure that his funeral was everything he wanted and everything my family would have expected. The funeral directors had assured me that my wishes would be carried out and it was so important to get it right. The hardest decision was the one I had to make for myself. We had been told that Liam had taken the shot in his lip so the facial injuries were extreme. They were right to warn me and I wasn't sure I wanted that to be the lasting image of my son that I carried in my head forever. So I made the decision not to view him, and the casket was closed when I got there. Some days I regret that decision and some days I don't. It didn't stop me going to him and talking to him every day up until the very last possible moment. I was going to take every opportunity to spend as much time on earth with my son as possible.

I suppose I have concentrated my memories of Liam on how he was when I last saw him and hugged him that day in February – larger than life and always smiling. Whenever I picture him in my mind there are things about him that never change and some that always make me smile and sometimes laugh out loud, which I do without thinking, and I can be in company at the time. I don't care if people think I'm mad. I'm just thinking of my son and that's how he was.

If you saw Liam in a T-shirt or his rugby shirt and jeans, you'd know he was happy. He was always more comfortable in his casuals and he had this habit of standing with his thumbs in his pockets – sometimes, if he was smoking, it would be just the one, but he always did it. That's how I remember him. And how I always will.

I gave the funeral directors the details of what I wanted them to do – with every attention to the detail. I said I wanted Liam to be dressed in his favourite T-shirt and jeans so he would be more comfortable, and he was to have his thumbs in his pockets. And I warned them that I had gathered a few things that must go in the coffin with him and that included a packet of ciga-rettes and his lighter. I said they must be in there because he never went anywhere without his smokes. Michael, my stepson, was so kind and offered me a packet of his cigarettes but I'm sorry to say that I cruelly rejected them with: 'No, Liam would never have smoked that rubbish!' I felt awful afterwards and I hope Michael understood that at this point I was a mother on a mission and everything had to be right and as if Liam had chosen everything himself. After all, I wasn't going to get another chance to do the best for my son.

My family and friends were fantastic. They were so helpful and understanding and let me get on with all my plans as I'm sure they realised that any attempt to stop me or talk me out of something was not going to work. There was one last thing I needed to hand to the funeral director, and that was my last letter to Liam. He wrote a final letter to me to say his goodbyes and so I wanted to do the same for him.

Writing to him in Afghan every day was easy. It made me feel so much better, as if we had chatted and everything was normal. I still have the unopened letter I wrote to him on the day he died. It was returned to me that way, so the letter I was about to write to him would be the first letter since then, and suddenly it didn't feel so easy any more.

Writing a goodbye letter to my own son was the most agonising thing I have ever done in my life. You would think it would be easier knowing that he was never going to read it or tell you if he got upset, but that's not how it was in my head at all. Saying goodbye to Liam in a letter was hard and made harder still knowing that it would be the very last letter, too. I can't share my words but I know it started like this … and I know I signed off as I always did.

Hiya son
Remember you said writing your letter to me was the hardest thing you've ever done well this letter to you is the hardest thing I've ever done.
    You are everything I could want in a son and a soldier …
    Stay safe son.
    Love you loads, Mum
xxxxxxxxxxxxxxxxxxxxxxxxxxx

The flowers, it turned out, were easily decided upon. We had agreed as a family that everyone joining us at the funeral would be honouring Liam the soldier, the man, the son, brother, grandson, uncle, nephew and partner. To everyone who knew Liam he was BLT – the dude. So there it was, in white carnations, for all to see – DUDE. He would have liked that, because it made people smile. That's what Liam always did. He made people smile. It was as if that's what he was on Earth to do.

He not only had a gift with dogs but he was blessed with the ability to connect with people, too. If you had met him you would never forget him.

My son could light up a room just by stepping into it and I wanted to make sure that side of Liam was there right to the end and never forgotten.

As the lone piper played I honestly thought my heart would burst. I saw Liam's friend, Karl Ingram, who was carrying my son for the second time, and I mouthed a 'thank you' to him as we gathered outside the church by the hearse. I had spoken to Karl at the repatriation and there he was again preparing to bear Liam on his shoulder. Leah wanted to make sure that the bearer party was made up of the men Liam had listed in his final letter. Karl had put his name forward for the job anyway, even before he knew that Liam had requested he carry his 'fat ass' twice. We were sad but we certainly knew we were amongst friends.

Liam's funeral was at 1.30pm to allow people travelling from afar to get there in good time, and it seemed that everyone made it. The church was packed to the rafters and there were crowds of local people and press spilling out into the churchyard. There were TV cameras at every turn. We were so grateful to the good people of Tayport who accommodated all the chaos we caused around the church most of the day. I was incredibly touched by their warmth and understanding.

After the service we discovered that the roads had been closed to allow the cars access to the cemetery, and just outside the gates, lined up ready to greet us as we came out, the children from Tayport primary school stood quietly with their heads bowed. It was so incredibly moving.

When the tears started and finished I have no idea. I don't think I cried the entire day because I remember Liam's bearers making sure that the gathering after the funeral was very much a 'celebration' of my son's life and not a wake. They really brought the house down when they took off their tunics and revealed their matching T-shirts bearing the legend 'Our Hero. Liam Tasker' above a photograph of Liam and Theo. They had been wearing them in his honour throughout the service.

There was plenty of alcohol consumed that day and plenty of stories shared about Liam, who I know some described as a 'Marmite character'. I can understand that because his serious side could be as strong as the joker inside him, but even for those who didn't see his funny side they still admired the man who trained a good dog to accomplish great things.

I think that was the most memorable message from the day – that Liam was good but with Theo they made each other great.

Lieutenant Colonel Chris Ham was present in Wootton Bassett and attended Liam's funeral. He had seen my son and Theo work closely together so it was good for me and for everyone to hear him sing their praises. I understood when he said that it's unusual for a dog to have one master in the Army and the pain it can cause when a bonded partnership is split for operational reasons. A dog can remain in theatre for two consecutive sixth-month tours but the handler will go home after one. That's when the dog will be handled by someone else. At least Liam and Theo didn't have to suffer the separation that Liam was dreading, and I believe they are together enjoying every day as they used to side by side. It helps me to have that picture in my head.

I still worry about Liam's friends. I can't help it. They are such a great bunch of people who made Liam's life so full of laughter and blokey banter. At the funeral I had the chance to meet some of the lads and lasses he had been mentioning in his phone calls and conversations over the years in the REME as well as the RAVC and I could tell that memories of my son weren't going to fade easily. They said lots of lovely things about him that made my heart sing: 'BLT … large as life with a heart of gold …' and Liam was '… a good mate, a good soldier and a perfectionist as a dog trainer. Theo was a cracking dog, and that said everything about Liam.' His friend Ryan Earnshaw said, 'Feels like we left a piece of the big man in Afghan. I miss him and he still owes me twenty quid!'

I couldn't help feeling sorry for Liam's girlfriend, Leah. She was beside us the whole time and she had her own pain to bear. They were very close and losing Liam was such a shock for the poor girl. She was the last person to speak to him on the Sunday before he died and they had been making plans for his home-coming, so there was lots of excitement about it all and then suddenly – nothing.

Leah also knew that Liam had been feeling a little bit down having to leave Theo in Afghan, but as she's a Royal Army Vet Corps nurse, with her own posting due, she understood a lot more of what goes on behind the scenes than the rest of us. I know she did her best to try to calm Liam and reassure him that Theo would be waiting for him when he got back. She knew how much that meant to him and I was grateful that she could step in and help him as he was very agitated about the whole thing. He wanted to come home but he didn't want to leave Theo. The bond had become that strong that I think Liam felt he was torn between leaving one family member to go and see others.

I will never forget what Leah told the papers after the funeral: 'I am the proudest girlfriend there could ever be and there will be a LT-sized hole in my life forever.' I cried for them both and I cried because I knew exactly what she meant. Nothing and no one would ever fill that gap. He was one of life's uniques, and so was Theo.

Chapter 15
Hero dogs

THEO

Two days after the body of Liam Tasker was repatriated to the UK the ashes of his faithful dog, Theo, were presented to Jane Duffy. Man and dog had made the journey together and it was Jane's wish that Theo's shell casing would find its final resting place at her son's feet. Just as he would have wanted, as it was the place where the dog had spent so many nights when they were on operations in the Afghan desert.

Liam Tasker wasn't into writing letters but a short time before he went on what was to be his final mission the young Lance Corporal started to pen a homage to his canine companion. He meant it to be a citation for an award that would show the world that his dog was a full-on, no-messing war dog. Full stop.

Liam clearly wanted Theo to receive some kind of formal recognition for his courage in conflict. In the five short months that he was in theatre the skilful spaniel located a record-breaking 14 operational 'finds' in one tour. The dog was known to be the best the RAVC could offer at the time, and one of the reasons why he was so very good was Liam Tasker. Everyone knew that and respected them both for all the lives saved as a result of their success. Every IED located, every haul of weapons and ammunition sniffed out was one less danger to the soldiers and to the local people. Death and life-changing injuries affected everyone in or out of a uniform.

Liam knew Theo was an extraordinary dog. His handwritten citation was ready to pass to his Commanding Officer when the tour was over: he would need their support if he intended to nominate Theo for the PDSA Dickin Medal – the Animals' Victoria Cross. That's what Liam wanted for his brave companion; nothing but the highest honour would do for his dog. Everyone he told about his plan for the medal was pleased and agreed that Theo deserved it. The Theo fan club was right behind the idea from day one.

Sadly, Liam and Theo didn't make it home, but thankfully the letter did.

A sheet of A4 lined paper, folded and folded again, probably to fit into a pocket or slip into his Bergen, carried Theo's story in scrawling black ink. You can't help thinking that Liam started to write down his thoughts about Theo while they were out on an operation, taking advantage of one of the many quiet moments of waiting and waiting in the desert, the dog stretched out at his feet.

It has the look of an unfinished document, as if Liam was just getting into his stride describing his incredible companion and his admiration for the dog he called his mate and his best friend: *'During all my Ops Theo has been absolutely amazing and works hard for me on every patrol which in turn has carried me through some difficult times. Even when covering over 18km in one day Theo was still raring to go all the way back to bed!'* He described Theo as a 'character', something Liam had been called many times himself. Maybe it was a case of two likeable rogues finding each other and giving their best?

Theo was Liam's hero but he was a hero to others, too. There were no medals given in the Green Zone of Afghanistan but if they had one to hand the Parachute Regiment would have slapped one on Theo's chest for sure. The man and dog were assigned to several Companies within 2 Para, including the Small Strike teams, which meant repeated daily patrols over a period of weeks. Living in dust craters in the desert, brushing through the lushness of the Green Zone and wading through the cool water of the life-giving Helmand River were everyday experiences for Theo. His insatiable high drive for the job combined with an unshakeable devotion to his handler gave the dog his unstoppable quality.

Deployed on hele assault operations throughout Helmand Province, Liam and Theo went forward, ahead of the patrol, to search for the bombs and weapons planted in order to kill and maim. Bustling around, stumpy tail wagging and quivering with excitement, Theo located everything set down to cripple the men and the mission. No wonder Theo was a dog the men soon grew to trust, and it was clear that, in their eyes, this dog who did it all for a chew on his favourite yellow ball was going beyond the call of duty every day of his tour.

In recognition of his soldiering and his life-saving skills the Parachute Regiment had extended their greatest honour, to award Theo his own Para Wings. Why? They said: 'He's one of us' – the dog who lived and worked to their motto: 'Ready for anything.' Theo accepted his wings with glossy black head held high.

Liam took the embroidered badge of honour and sewed it to Theo's harness. The harness also bore his RAVC tactical recognition flash (horizontal stripes of dark blue, yellow and maroon), which Theo also wore with pride and military bearing. It was as if the nifty black and white spaniel was fully aware, by some miracle of dog sense, that he was wearing battle honours. After the mini-presentation ceremony he visited each of the soldiers present with a friendly sniff and wiggle and then set himself at his master's feet as if to say: 'OK, that was fun, but what's next then, boss?'

The well-folded 'pen picture' Liam started to write was found amongst his papers at Camp Bastion. He left his last letter to his mother and to members of his family. To Theo he left a legacy that would ensure he was not only internationally recognised as a dog of war but would go down in history as a life-saving hero of the Afghan conflict. On 25 October 2012, Royal Army Veterinary Corps arms and explosives search dog Theo was awarded a posthumous PDSA Dickin Medal: *'For outstanding gallantry and devotion to duty while deployed with 104 Military Working Dog (MWD) Squadron during the conflict in Afghanistan in September 2010 to March 2011.'*

The poignant ceremony at the Wellington Barracks in London was hosted by animal lover Paul O'Grady, the family's choice of celebrity, whose own deep respect for the animal kingdom was clear to see. He, like most of the invited guests, failed to hold back tears as the short film depicting the life and times of Liam and Theo was played out to the room. The footage had been captured shortly before Liam and Theo died and it showcased their skills and those of every other dog and handler serving. The bond between the soldier and the dog was evident; every move and every word in praise of them as individuals and as a life-saving team.

Sergeant Matt Jones, RAVC, who had served with Liam in Afghanistan, handled AES dog Grace, the dog chosen to accept the medal on Theo's behalf. A new recruit herself with a tour of duty ahead of her, the small, marble-black spaniel wore Theo's Dickin Medal with pride.

Sadly, Liam wasn't there to see his beloved dog collect the honour that he wanted so much for him, but the letter he left behind ensured that the award was made with his blessing and, literally, with his name attached. They had both been living the dream – and the dream came true.

SASHA

It was Frank Holmes who decided that it was time to nominate Sasha for an award to recognise her lifesaving courage in conflict. The research for this book uncovered many people who agreed with Frank and, six years after the loss of Ken, many felt that enough time had passed to heal the scars and were able to talk about that time again. It is fair to say that there were others who felt their memories of Helmand Province in July 2008 were still too raw to revisit. They preferred to keep their still-writhing demons buried a while longer. But if there was one thing that everyone Frank consulted agreed on, it was that it was time to salute Sasha.

Back in 2008, when Sasha was deployed to Afghanistan, she was the dog that stood out from the crowd. Marianne Hay had made sure that she had trained her well and that she was a savvy sniffer dog who not only had the skills to make the grade but to exceed expectations. She was the dog everyone wanted to get their hands on – the Taliban included.

The 'yellow dog' was good at her job and that's why Ken Rowe asked for her. As the dog with a confirmed 15 operational 'finds' over her time in Afghanistan, Sasha had set the standard for all others to follow. It was in Musa Qala that Andy Dodds saw, first hand, the quality of Sasha as a search dog. In the heart of the Taliban's 'spiritual homeland' Sasha regularly foiled the insurgents' plans by locating caches of arms and ammunition and she proved that she had a keen sense for uncovering the new weapon of choice, the IED. She continued the trend of success in Garmsir, where the network of sinister underground tunnels and trenches was no hiding place when Sasha was around. Deadly explosive devices, rocket-propelled grenade motors and bomb components were all uncovered before they could kill or maim.

Frank's nomination for Sasha to receive a posthumous PDSA Dickin Medal was supported by Lt Col Chris Ham, the military hierarchy and numerous eyewitness accounts. Her extraordinary success as an arms and explosives search dog resulted in the saving of many, many lives and her lifesaving courage in conflict earned Sasha the highest honour.

On 21 May 2014 her former handler, Sergeant Major Andy Dodds, accompanied Fire, a retired IED detection dog, who accepted Sasha's medal at a special ceremony at Kensington Town Hall in London. Fire, a Black Labrador, was well qualified for the job. An Afghanistan veteran, she was injured when an IED exploded close to her but she survived against the odds thanks to the expert care of the RAVC veterinary surgeons and nurses at Camp Bastion and then back home at Melton Mowbray.

It was a poignant occasion celebrating the life and sacrifice of Sasha, one very brave dog who died alongside a brave soldier. Many of the guests were those who had, in some way, been involved in Sasha's story, which had ended all too soon in the heat and dust of a conflict so very far from home. Naturally, Lyn and her family were there to share in the events of the day: 'Kenneth and Sasha spent their last moments together so she will always be regarded as special to us. My son knew she was a gifted dog but never forgot that she was still a dog and always forgave her for chasing the odd cat or chicken when she got the chance. She wasn't perfect, but for him she was the best at the job. He felt safe with her and knew he could trust her because once that working harness was on she was his dog. Kenneth would have liked to think that Sasha had been awarded a medal. If he was watching over the ceremony, which I believe he was, he would have been so proud of her.'

Chapter 16

Coping beyond hope

LYN

How? Just keep going ...

After the dreadful news that Kenneth had been killed in action, then the horror of the repatriation and the finality of the funeral there came this dreadful ... silence.

Suddenly everything that was anything to do with my son over the last few months of his life had been reduced to a few random cardboard boxes. Life in the Forces creates a necessity to travel light but at the end of it all there didn't seem much left. And Kenneth liked his 'things' and he liked 'stuff', so it was odd, to say the least, to be sorting a few items of clothing, some left-over toiletries, notepaper and pens.

I knew that Iain Carnegie and Mark Atkinson had taken on the unenviable task of gathering Kenneth's belongings together. I really did feel for them. What a dreadful job to have to pack up your friend's room. I hope it isn't too distressing for them. At least Iain and Mark knew my son and I knew that they would take a lot of care doing the job and boxing it all for its return to us.

It was a grim thing opening that first box. The house already had so many photographs of Kenneth and his various military dogs all over and, although we had moved his room to give Stephanie the bigger space, his 'new' room was laid out ready for him. He was due home so I wanted him to be able to step in through the front door and just go to bed with all his familiar things around him. Now I had more to add to the collection but without the joy of knowing he would be seeing it all.

The sand got into everything. There was the book, *The Golden Compass*. That's where they found Kenneth's last letter to me. He had written it and used it as a bookmark and maybe there was some sense in that as he probably knew that it would be discovered if it was ever needed. As he had written on the envelope, 'For the eyes of Lyn Rowe only', it would have been clear to most people that it was a special letter, not something meant for the waste bin. I loved the envelope, made from a random sheet of paper and held together with sticky tape. Kenneth was quite fussy and liked things to be right so it must have irked him to see how the sand had found its way into every fold of the paper and under the tape. There really was no escaping it.

Then there were the magazines sent all the way from Newcastle: copies of the *Auto Traders* supplied by his dad and the letters from me. They were all there, with a coating of the Afghan desert. His fatigues and helmet were there, too, and other pieces of equipment that he would have had with him for the repatriation to the UK. Everything I touched I knew Kenneth had touched out there. When I picked up a book or a letter it had the smell of dry stones and grit. And when I moved the first box to one side it left a trail of orange sand on the cream carpet.

Out of the silence of those days after Kenneth's death came one of the most amazing and surprising sources of strength. So many letters of condolence poured through our letterbox and many of them were from total strangers who had seen the news on the television or in the papers and wanted to connect with me and my family. It was incredibly overwhelming.

I had a letter from an elderly lady who was a wife and mother, and after hearing about Kenneth she just wanted to reach out and take my hand. Believe me, when your son is killed by uncaring terrorists and you're convinced that the world is a vile place with no good in it you need people like that to restore your faith in human nature. For her to go to the trouble to write was very touching. I have kept that letter and always will.

For some reason I expected the letters from the Army to be stark in tone and content but I couldn't have been more wrong. To lose one of their own who was so young had clearly hit them hard. Every letter spoke of Kenneth's 'professionalism, dedication, self-lessness and integrity' and, most importantly to me, his mother, what a lovely person he was to have around.

As mothers we need to know that our children are liked by their peers and that they are never going to be the child that's bullied or excluded just because they are 'different'. The fear is that if they are that unfortu-nate child we are not always going to be there to protect them and life will be hard. No mother wants that. But I know Kenneth's life was good. And when it wasn't so good we made it better. That's what parents do, isn't it? But even if we could turn back time I wouldn't have stopped him doing the job he loved and that made him happy. We could not have saved him and, more than that, he wouldn't have wanted us to.

After we lost Kenneth many of his friends wrote to me or called the house to pass on their condolences. My son was only 24 years old but he had touched so many lives and I thought it was lovely and brave of them to contact us and share their feelings. He was clearly more of a lovable rogue than we saw at home, and tales of 'the legendary Karaoke Ken' and his unforgettable rendition of 'Great Balls of Fire' were just hilarious. I remember him being obsessed with having knife-edge creases in everything but then I heard how he had taken this into his Army life – much to the amusement of his mates. But out of all of this came one lovely common theme and that was that Kenneth was always talking about his family. Many of them felt they knew us because they had heard so much about us. That really made me smile inside. 'The cheeky Geordie with a smile for everyone ... A high-calibre soldier, dedicated dog handler and talented sportsman who was destined for great things in the Army ...' That was my son.

Hearing all these good words about my son made the coping easier, but it just didn't seem real. Surely people were talking about someone else's boy? Someone who sounded very like Kenneth but not him. My mind leaped between the truth and denial of the truth all the time. The only thing that seemed to stop the cycle was work. So I immersed myself in that. Coping soon became connected to long hours. I worked to take my mind off it as much as was humanly possible. If I worked, then it couldn't catch up with me. If I kept working I would always be ahead of the next wave of panic and hopelessness.

The shockwaves of Kenneth's death rippled through the Newcastle community, and particularly in West Moor/Killingworth where we live and where Kenneth went to school and played most of his sport. It seemed to me that the feeling of disbelief that was running through our family had extended into the homes and families around us. I suppose Kenneth's death had brought what was happening in Afghanistan closer than the daily newspaper or the TV news could as it was now on our neighbours' doorsteps.

I appreciated that they would maybe not remember the soldier; instead they might remember the Ken Rowe they knew, and that could have been from the time he worked at Asda. Some of them might be thinking of the young lad who decided he was going to help with the fashion show in aid of a breast cancer charity and ended up volunteering to 'strut his stuff' on the catwalk wearing pink boxers! It's possible they would remember him raising money for a scanner at the local Freeman Hospital following the death of his school friend from sudden cardiac death syndrome. He didn't need any persuading to do this kind of thing. It's who he was.

It felt as if our kind friends were wrapping us up in something warm and protective to weather our storm, and the many creative projects and memorials they had in mind were a reassurance that Kenneth would never be forgotten. It was something we needed, although at the time I couldn't really believe they were talking about my son. It wasn't real. Everyone was so very, very kind, and it was wonderful to see people being so positive at a time that felt so uncertain and confusing for all of us.

My girls were finding it hard to cope with the loss of their brother who was also their best friend. When Kenneth left us it created a huge gap in our lives, and the loss reached into our extended family.

All I can remember of that time after the funeral was hoping that some time very soon we would all wake up from the dreadful nightmare and go and collect Kenneth from Brize Norton where he would be waiting for us to take him home. When I realised that was never going to happen I went into coping mode, my self-made world where I could work and be mother to Jeni and Steph, wife to Ken, grandmother to Riley, Tai and Hannah and stay on that track. No deviation or time lapses to think beyond the 'must-do' things. If I allowed myself to wander from this path I knew I would be lost. Kenneth had become a father to beautiful Hannah while he was in Afghanistan. He never made it home to see his daughter. This is the greatest sadness for me because he wanted to see her so very much and every letter since her birth in March 2008 included a mention of her: 'Mam, have you seen the baby? How's the baby? She's beautiful isn't she, Mam?' Kenneth grew up in the last weeks of his tour; even his letters hinted at a more responsible version of our Kenneth. It's such a pity he never had the chance to be Hannah's father. But now, at seven years old, she is showing so many what we call 'Kennethisms'. Little things she says are as he would say them and certain expressions are his to a T. She smiles and everyone smiles with her. Her daddy would be so proud of her.

In October 2014 Hannah had an idea. Her mother bought her a poppy for the Remembrance Day service but when they got home Hannah decided it needed a little something to make it extra special to remember her daddy. Armed with glue and glitter she glitzed the poppies and then, seeing how lovely they were, she glitzed some more! She took a simple Remembrance poppy and made it fit for her hero – her daddy.

JANE

Liam wasn't only a soldier, he was my son too, and I miss him more than words can say. He ended his final letter to the family by saying: 'Each day is a gift, not a given right,' and I believe that too.

What you're left with at the end of the day, after the funeral and the soulful bleat of the lone piper still in your head, are the letters, photographs, memories and the pain of loss. You can wallow in it if you want to. I didn't come across anyone brave enough to try to stop me and, besides, it's perfectly real and understandable. But when you have other children still looking to you to make things happen I realised that I needed to pull in all that emotion and consider the future.

When I looked ahead to the years without Liam I didn't visualise a very happy place. Many times I said to myself, 'What's the point?' But I was still a mother to Laura, Ian and Nicola. They had not only shared in my grief, they had suffered in their own ways, too, and they needed me now more than ever. I didn't need to be Super Mum but by God I needed to be something close to it.

Nicola had taken the news about Liam really badly. She was only 13 years old and I'm sure it never entered her head that being in the Army and in a war zone could end up with him not making it home. Liam was always there for Nic; even when he was miles away he would call her and cheer her up. He was her big brother and she loved him to bits.

I know it probably sounds very strange but we didn't really notice right away how quiet and withdrawn Nic had become. At first I thought it was just her being so young and finding it hard to handle such huge emotions but then I realised that she wasn't speaking at all. When I took her to the doctor he said that there didn't seem to be any physical reason why she could have trouble speaking but then asked if she had experienced any stress in her life recently. It didn't seem right that a young girl of Nicola's age should be stressed about anything so without thinking I heard myself saying, 'No, nothing, although it has been a bit difficult at home recently as her brother was killed in Afghanistan.' I think he looked at me as if I didn't know the definition of stress. Hearing this, his conclusion was that Nicola had most likely been literally struck dumb through grief.

It took some time for her to start speaking again, and the grief still affects her from time to time. Even now she will sometimes avoid going out and she always goes shopping at the quiet times to avoid crowds. That kind of thing still unsettles her a great deal. Liam would hate to think that his little sis was suffering like that. He would have helped her over it for sure and found a way to make her laugh. He would have been very proud of her this summer as she gained the exam success she needed to take up a place at university. I can imagine his face gleaming when I told him that and that his 'little but big sister', Laura, has decided to start teacher training. To me it shows their great strength in the face of adversity and maybe a little of the power of miracles.

An object, an anniversary, a memory, a photograph, a chance remark – anything like that can really kick it off. I was OK in my bubble of grief until something broke through the very thin membrane and then I was lost, sometimes for days.

It was about three months after the funeral that Sergeant Major Adrian Davies delivered the boxes of Liam's belongings that came in from Camp Bastion and North Luffenham. I didn't know what to do with them. They stood in the hall for days. Jimmy was concerned, I could tell, and the girls, too.

I could have cried with relief when my brother and his wife offered to take them and store them in their garage for me, at least until we could come up with a better idea. Part of me didn't want them moved because, to me, they were a part of Liam that was home, but I knew they had to go somewhere. It was while I was helping to move them out that I lifted one that felt so light that I thought it must be empty. No point in storing an empty box, I thought. I handed it to Lynne for a second opinion, and she thought the same, so I decided to open it to be sure. When Adrian handed everything over to me he said something about the kind of things I could find in the boxes and that if there was any paperwork it would have had holes punched in it but that was just standard procedure and nothing to worry about. I could only imagine it was something like that in there, if anything at all. I just didn't want any more surprises or things to worry about. I felt calm, actually, very calm, but with a few butterflies in the bottom of my stomach … just in case.

I stripped back the sticky tape and lifted the lid. There lay Liam's sand goggles and camelback (water bottle). He would have had them with him on the day he died. I suddenly realised that Liam was in that box. I slammed my hand down on it and taped it shut. I ran my hand over the top and remembered how good my son looked skipping along in his uniform and how proud he was to have Theo by his side. It's who Liam was, and I will always picture him and imagine him standing tall and handsome next to me ... just as he was in the last photograph we had together.

Letters and keepsakes mean everything when you can't touch and speak to the person you love any more. I was lucky to have been given some of my most treasured possessions around the time of Liam's funeral – one of them being his wallet. It came in a small box with some paperwork and looked as if it had been freshly collected from the desert floor.

It was curled at the corners, most likely because it had been carried in his breast pocket and had curved to the shape of his chest. I'm not sure how long I sat there stroking the soft brown leather – probably ages – but when I eventually opened it out a cascade of sand ran from its creases onto my dark skirt.

There was hardly anything in it. Typical Liam, getting by on the least possible baggage. But then I remembered that he would not have been able to carry anything that identified him should he or the wallet fall into enemy hands. There was a photograph of him with some friends and a note from a mate to say he owed them a few 'crates' (of beer) – his penance for having his and Theo's faces splashed all over the papers in February. There was a little bit of money, enough for a few drinks when he got back to Camp Bastion, I'm sure, and a letter. I wanted to read that bluey so badly but another part of me held back. If he carried this with him what did it say, and if it was from Leah, his girlfriend, it was not for me to read. I'm not that kind of mother. It was his business, not mine. I agonised but curiosity got the better of me.

The thin sheet of blue airmail paper had been folded in several places to make it fit snugly into the wallet and its creases were deep and darkened. It must have been read and re-read a million times. As I pinched it out of the wallet to take a proper look a few more grains of sand spilled out of its folds and it happened again as I turned it to read the sender's address in the top left-hand corner: the letter was from me. I caught my breath.

Wednesday 3 October
Hiya Son,

I hope you're feeling better. I'm so glad that you got your parcel. I honestly thought it had been confiscated. That would be just my luck.

I'm going to ring you on Friday to see if you are any better. Your Auntie Shelagh and Uncle Bernie are coming over next Tuesday for the October Fest. That should be a good night. I saw Jamie this morning and asked him if he was still OK to babysit. He said 'yes' thank God! He goes into the RAF in Nov (NO SMART REMARKS THANK YOU).

Dad has had a phone call and should get his Chief Tech in the next few weeks. I'm really pleased for him. At last eh??!! Ian was saying he's off to Bosnia. I don't quite know how I'm feeling about that. It's bad enough you both being in the Army in the UK but any further is a nightmare to me. I really miss you son and I can't wait until Christmas when I see you again. As long as you're happy though. That's all that matters. It's your life at the end of the day.

I forgot to tell you I've moved your room. You're now in the room Nicola used to be in. It looks really good. I've even put some of your posters up for you. Another thing – we've got a new telly so once you're at Arborfield you'll be OK for a telly in your room.

Anyway that's about it for now. The girls are fine. Still arguing and what have you, but what's new eh?

I really hope you're feeling better son. Remember, keep smiling, don't let them get you down NO MATTER WHAT! Love and miss you loads son. Take care. God bless. Love and kisses.

Mum xxxxxxxxxxx

My chest and my throat hurt.

The letter was ten years old. It was probably the first letter I wrote to him when he joined up and left home. And he had kept it. Why that particular letter I don't know as it was full of the usual drivel. I shocked myself with the rubbish I put in those letters. The poor boy must have wondered what on earth I was going on about. I just wanted him to get the news from home. I never imagined it would be something he would carry with him all the time. I was deeply touched by it. I like to think it was his way of having his family with him all the time. Thank God for those bloody fabulous blueys.

I re-folded the letter, which had caught my tears, and put it back in Liam's wallet. I sat with that sun-bleached bit of leather in my hands for some time. I felt somehow hypnotised by it. I closed my eyes and remembered the many times I had seen it lying around the house and how many times I had rescued it from pockets of trousers and shirts destined for the washing machine. I assumed that it would have been one of the last things that Liam held on his last day, maybe even in his last hours in Afghan. Now there I was sitting holding the same wallet at home, but without him. It wasn't right. Nothing about it was right.

When I was given Liam's beret and Theo's harness I knew I was holding the two items with the power to bring Liam and his beloved dog alive again – to me, anyway. My son was always so proud to wear that beret and I know he would have been true to his regiment to the end. He lived and breathed the Army. And Theo's worn and dusty harness fixed and handled by Liam who made sure Theo's regimental flash and Para Wings were always proudly on view – his badge of honour. Liam's dad has the beret now and the harness is in my care. I wear my son's dog tag every day with an angel's wing beside it.

If only Theo had lived to wear his Dickin Medal. I would have liked that and I would have seen it as a shared award for Liam and Theo for being all they were to each other. Liam loved that dog and was so proud of him that he had left that nomination for Theo to have a medal to recognise his record number of fourteen finds in one tour in Afghanistan, a record that still stands. All achieved in the face of conflict. If they had lived, they would have been friends for life, and one thing I believe for sure is that they are together now.

One of the greatest lasting gifts I have of my son and that dog he loved so much is a DVD made by Liam himself. He edited together the best of the images and videos of the two of them with the perfect backing track: 'You've got a friend in me' from the film *Toy Story*. It's absolutely fantastic, and when I'm feeling a bit low I know it's something that will cheer me up, and if it makes me cry instead, then at least I've had my 'fix'. I need that from time to time. The only thing I need to remember is to stop it before the end because the final scene carries the words: 'That's all folks ... until next time.' And of course there will never be a next time.

I remember after Liam was killed I thanked Theo in my head for keeping my son safe. I know this might sound daft to people but it doesn't to me, and remember it wasn't an IED that got my son, and that was thanks to Theo. If that great dog could have stood in the way of that fatal bullet I'm sure he would have done. He loved his master that much.

Chapter 17

Moving on

LYN

Before any of this happened to us if someone had asked me what despair felt like I would have given the best description I could of an unfathomable feeling of loss and hopelessness. But I can tell you now there is a place way beyond despair and I know because I've been there.

When you hit the bottom there really is only one way to go and that's back up. I've heard that said so many times, and I've probably said it to a lot of people, too – because I believe it's true. I've never presumed that my pain has been more debilitating than the next person's because we all have our bad times and pain is relative, but I think it's how we choose to deal with loss that can make or break us.

Moving on has just happened day by day. I go to work, I cook and clean and I'm there for my husband, my daughters and my grandchildren. And Kenneth?

I'm there for him, too. He is still in our lives in so many ways. For a long time after his death I would go shopping and buy his favourite things. I wouldn't realise until I got home and unpacked everything that I had shopped on automatic pilot. It used to upset me, but not now. Now I get scared and upset if I discover that I haven't bought something for him because I think I could be forgetting him or at least accepting that I'm moving on without him. I honestly didn't think that was possible but I'm finding I can cope after all.

I say that, but still admit that I'm haunted by things said or unsaid while Kenneth was alive. I think we both possess a sixth sense. The irony is, I think he had the same gift because we both 'sensed' things were going to happen. I know my son had a bad feeling on the morning he was killed. It's difficult for people to understand that kind of thing if it's not something they share or believe in but for people like Kenneth and myself it is real and when it's attached to fear it's very real indeed.

I'm not saying he could have been saved or anything like that; I know it doesn't work that way and I know Kenneth wouldn't have wanted to be anywhere other than doing his job alongside 2 Para. I'm just saying that the thought of him sensing something dark was hanging over him still haunts me. I can't help that. I have visions of him sitting in the desert, Sasha at his side and both of them covered in sand, the Taliban lying in wait. I'm convinced that's why I couldn't concentrate that day and couldn't sleep that night. It felt as if I was being kept awake for a reason. We were expecting Kenneth home but he stayed to do his job and I'm so proud of my son for doing what he did and staying on to protect his mates. He acted with care and honour and the Army and his family could not have asked for more. I just wish he had been on his way home.

Steps forward and steps back, that's how I see moving on from Kenneth's death. Each day I still wake up with a deep sense of loss and as the day wears on the feeling wears away, but it never really goes that far from me. It only takes one tiny reminder to set me back to where I started. Anything can do it – cleaning out Trevor the tortoise, a photo found in a book, a kind comment from a friend or maybe his favourite mug finds its way to the front of the cupboard … lots of everyday things. Sometimes if I make the mistake of spending a little longer than is good for me in Kenneth's room I risk taking a step back.

Everything of his is in there, except for the framed photographs we have on the stairs and landing. I know some would call his room a shrine, and maybe it is, in a way, but we use it as a guest room, too, so it's still a 'living' part of the house. I like going in there. It's where I can sit amongst Kenneth's things, things he touched and treasured, like his go-karting memorabilia and Newcastle United match programmes and beloved football shirts … all there. I can pretend for a while and tell myself that he'll be home later or just chat to him, catch up on things that are bothering him. It helps. It has always helped.

Remembering the good times always helps, even if there are tears somewhere along the line. We have so many photographs of Kenneth as a child and in all of them he is smiling. From his first photograph as a baby right through to the last ones of him with his mates in Afghanistan he was smiling. Regrets come into the frame sometimes, but mostly I concentrate on remembering the good times and all those smiles.

As I immersed myself in my work, Ken and the girls stumbled their way through their own grieving process. Ken, our rock, was always there to catch us if we fell. Quiet, stoic and amazing, he grieved for his son but always put our pain ahead of his own. I don't know what we would have done without him. Jeni and Steph clung to us and we worked it out together so they were able to move on with their lives in the wake of Kenneth's death. They had lost their brother – my middle child – and it wasn't just their own friends they needed for support, they appreciated contact from Kenneth's friends, too.

I'm not a massive fan of Facebook myself, but the girls found it really useful as they tried to come to terms with what had happened to their brother. He had died such a violent death so far from home and without the people he loved at his side. Reaching out to his friends seemed to be the only tangible answer to trying to get close to where Kenneth fell. One of the Danish Army dog handlers that Kenneth had worked alongside as part of the combined operations in Afghanistan kept in contact with Jeni.

The young soldier had got on with Kenneth very well and knew all about us through the letters and parcels we used to send and Kenneth used to share with the guys. He knew what family meant to Kenneth and how much more we all came to mean to him out there where being shot at was an everyday hazard. As dog handlers they faced these fears together, and the bond was strong. We know from his messages to Jeni that there was massive respect for Kenneth as a dog handler (he received the gift of an Afghan rug from the Danes in recognition of his work with them) and a friend, and they obviously had the same sense of humour. Hearing from this young man was like hearing from a version of Kenneth – so comforting. He was very upset when he heard of Kenneth's death and later in the summer of 2008 we heard that this Danish soldier had lost his life out there, too. Poor Jeni was thrown by this news. As I said, moving on for us has often been a case of taking one step forward and two steps back.

It took two years for the inquest into Kenneth's death to be heard and I don't think any of us moved on too far until that was over. It was such an ordeal reliving the whole thing and hearing different people describe what happened and building a picture of that moment when we weren't there for him. When it was over I was exhausted in a way I didn't think possible. It was partly due to the build-up to the inquest which I hoped would answer all my questions because I wanted answers. Why did Kenneth die? What happened when he was hit? Was he in pain? Did anyone help him? What was the last thing he said? I knew I was asking too much and I had to accept that I wouldn't get all the answers. This was the Army and Kenneth was a soldier fighting a war. The verdict – death while on active service – was delivered on 23 September 2010.

People shouldn't have regrets, but I do. My regret is not asking more questions during the pre-inquest meeting. I needed to because a part of me still can't and won't accept what happened to Kenneth. He was a fit, healthy young man when I last saw him alive. When he came home to me he was in a coffin. As the mother with a son in the Armed Forces I was half prepared for the bad but somehow you still don't expect it. I have grown to accept that my son has gone because he is not here to speak to, cook for, buy gifts for, laugh with and take his next steps in life. But sometimes 24 July 2008 seems like only yesterday.

One of the massive, tangible supports in the moving-on process is the lasting knowledge that Kenneth was liked, respected and even loved by those who were his friends and colleagues in uniform. The very many letters of condolence we received after Kenneth's death remain a source of strength to me. I don't reach for them often but I know they are there if I ever need to be reassured that I brought a lovely man into the world. The words of friends and work colleagues eased the pain enormously. Everyone who had witnessed the cheeky little boy grow into the cheeky young man were happy to share their lasting memories with me and we had many laughs remembering all his antics over the years.

In the end everything comes back to the Army and the day he went beyond the call of duty and didn't make it home. There are so many times you can say 'if only' but the fact is Kenneth was where he wanted to be and doing what he wanted to do. He was a soldier and his dog, Sasha was a fellow soldier, and they died doing a soldier's job. Neither would have wanted it any other way. I know that but when I reach for one of the many military letters of condolence I have no doubts whatsoever that Kenneth's death was not in vain.

From Brigadier M. A. P. Carleton-Smith OBE
Commander
Headquarters 16 Air Assault Brigade
Task Force Helmand
Lashkar Gah
British Forces Post Office 715
Saturday 26 July 2008

Dear Mr and Mrs Rowe
It is with a heavy heart that I write to you both
to say how terribly sorry I am that Ken has been
killed. It is the news that we all dread and the
pain, shock and disbelief for you all must be
consuming and hard to bear.

But I want you to know that Ken was
much loved, admired and respected here too by
his many friends who were proud to call him
their mate. They all share your loss and your
grief and you are all very much in their
thoughts too. But whilst we have lost a fine,
brave and well-liked friend and colleague, you
have lost your son and nothing can replace him.
You are left instead with the memories of the
laughter, conversations and good times together
that made up for a lifetime – he lived it to the
full. If there is any small crumb of comfort it is
that Ken died doing a job that he loved
surrounded by his friends. He died a soldier's

death, on the battlefield. A warrior in life, as so when he died.

We are proud of him and all that he achieved and stood for. I know that you all share that pride. It now just remains for us all to be as brave as he always was – I know it will be hard and painful but I also know that the strength of your family will help you through.

Ken had courage – he must have got it from somewhere so it must run in the family.

With my deepest sympathy to you all.

Yours sincerely,

Mark Carleton-Smith OBE

Retired servicemen and veteran RAVC handlers wrote to express their sympathy. For many the announcement of Kenneth's death in the newspapers and on television brought back memories of their own colleagues lost in a fight against terrorism in Northern Ireland. Letters came in from people who had trained or been in training with Kenneth. I remember one saying how they had been on a walk with him and they remembered a 'proud young lad chatting and smiling' and being struck by 'what a likeable young lad he was'.

One of Kenneth's teachers who taught at the George Stephenson High School recognised the name of his former pupil on the news and picked up a pen to tell us about the boy he remembered teaching; a boy 'full of energy and enjoyment of life … such a bright, capable, lively lad – you always knew he was in the class. When they said on the news that he could have come home but chose to stay on duty, that fitted so clearly with my memory. In football or basketball he would be so passionate and determined and at any time he would stand up for what he thought was right. Stubborn and bloody minded you could call it – I think I did a few times.

'I remember a trip to the Lake District with lads from the tutor group and I think I almost came to blows with Kenneth at 2am when they wouldn't go to sleep. Oh well, that's Kenneth, right at the heart of things … These memories are a tiny fraction of those that others will share with you – and nothing compared to what you will carry inside yourselves – but I wanted to say that I am so sorry and will continue to remember a fine boy who clearly became a great man.'

Just recently the school honoured Kenneth by including him in their new GSHS Heroes Revealed programme. We were so pleased to be invited along to meet the students who had nominated Kenneth and Sasha to appear on one of the cards, which were presented to recognise positive work during 2015. I'm sure it wasn't the first time Kenneth's photograph appeared in the school magazine but it would have been the first as a soldier and local hero.

The youngsters had called Kenneth their most popular hero although they had bigger names listed to feature on their set of smart blue cads. National figures such as Sir Bobby Robson, Nelson Mandela, Neil Armstrong and Florence Nightingale were amongst them. Kenneth would have been delighted to see his name alongside Newcastle United footballing legend Jackie Milburn for sure. To see the children holding the cards with Kenneth and Sasha's photograph on really made my heart leap. My son would have loved to think he was being honoured in such a way. I told them that he would always be our hero and thanked them for making him theirs.

Since his death we've been told so many times that he was a great friend and soldier and we have always known that he was a wonderful son. Here or gone, Kenneth will always be my hero. If his life and career inspire others to do their best, not just for themselves but for others too, then it's the greatest thing that can come out of a devastating loss. I hope his life and career inspire others to do their best because that's the best thing that can come out of a bad situation.

We never split Kenneth's death from losing Sasha, so when she was posthumously awarded the PDSA Dickin Medal in May 2014 we were overjoyed to see her being honoured. I can hear Kenneth say now that he would have been 'minted' to see the courageous Lab accept her medal with pride. Sadly, it wasn't meant to be and, without Sasha or Kenneth, we attended the ceremony in London and watched the film of Sasha's canine colleagues being put through their paces and those who served with Kenneth talk about the close bond between the man and the dog. It reminded me that my son didn't die alone. He didn't have his family at his side but he had the next best thing – his canine protector.

We saw Andy Dodds help Fire (the 'stand-in' Sasha), accept the medal and thought it was right as Andy had handled Sasha just before Kenneth. But I couldn't help feeling sadness, particularly for Marianne Hay, who had trained the dog to such a high standard for her work. I'm sure she was proud of her little search dog and all she had achieved and I'm pleased that it was Marianne who was given the honour of taking Sasha's ashes to scatter. How we all wished that dog could have been there to collect her own reward for exceptional bravery at Kenneth's side.

When we got home to Newcastle we added the programme from Sasha's medal ceremony to the collection of Kenneth's treasures. As I placed the booklet in the box and put the certificate and citation to one side for hanging on the wall, I noticed the newspaper cutting from the *Sunday Telegraph* dated 27 July 2008. The reporter met Kenneth who was patrolling with B Company, 2 Para, into the Green Zone just days before the Taliban attack that took Kenneth and

Sasha from us. I like the article because it captures a slice of a day with Kenneth and the 30 other men in the patrol doing the job they loved in what was then one of the most dangerous places in the world. I sat and read it again, as I've done many times before and since.

The reporter was drawn to Sasha – the only bit of normality in a crazy place. Kenneth said that always happened when visitors or new units came into Bastion or a FOB: they always zoned in on Sasha and she was always happy to assume the role of much-loved soldiers' pet. This time she was in the proverbial dog house after giving in to her canine instincts and chasing one of the feral cats from the base! I think Kenneth knew Sasha pretty well by this time and knew she would be right back and ready to say sorry in her own way. Almost immediately realising she had done wrong, she gave up the cat and came to sit next to Kenneth, leaning into him for the pat that said: 'I forgive you.'

If Kenneth hadn't been killed that article would have been what I assume it was meant to be – a war correspondent's report on the challenges faced by the British soldiers in the killing field of Helmand Province. It was all of that, but it was tinged with an incredible sadness that the man and dog he had been talking to only days before were now dead. Kenneth had been killed before the story had been submitted for publication. The journalist was clearly in shock, as we were. People get killed in war but we somehow don't expect it to be the people we have just been speaking to, laughing with and walking alongside.

Every time I read that article and remember shaking the journalist's hand at Kenneth's funeral, I'm reminded that death is arbitrary. It did not choose Kenneth or Sasha. They were in Afghanistan doing their job and doing it well but it didn't make them invincible. They faced the same fears and dangers as every other soldier out there. That day they just didn't come home, and we have to live with that.

How am I living with it? As well as can be expected. Home today still includes the reminders of Kenneth. We still celebrate his birthday in October and we still roll out his favourite meals and I still expect Kenneth to walk through the door on baking days. If he was home he'd never miss the chance to grab what he could from the kitchen before it was offered!

And Christmas? That's just the best of all. We still do the full menu as Kenneth loved. One year he couldn't make up his mind which roast he wanted (because he loved every kind of Sunday roast we had) and said: 'All of them, Mam!' So that's what I did and still do – five joints of meat, including turkey. Now it's become a meal in his honour and we have a proper printed menu with the three choices of starter, five roasts with five different vegetables, followed by a selection of three puddings, then coffee and mints. He would have loved that.

When I do the menu I always remember the things he liked to eat and the things he loathed. One pudding Kenneth would never have eaten was rice pudding – not even for a laugh. One of the dinnerladies at his school made him eat it once even though he said he would be sick. True to his word, he was sick! His favourite was always apple pie with melted ice cream. We keep that on the menu every year, and it doesn't make me sad, it makes me really happy. I can see him now sitting at the table wolfing it down while watching everyone else's choices just to make sure there would be enough left for second helpings!

They say that moving house can be a very traumatic thing to do and I've been putting it off for a long time even though the girls now have homes of their own. We just need extra room for our grandsons Tai and Riley and our granddaughter Hannah when they come to stay. I'm ready for it now. It just feels like the right thing to do. It will be a big change for us and there are big decisions to make. Right now we have Kenneth's ashes in the hall – I moved them from the dining room as we thought it was heartless to have him watch us eat all his favourite meals. They will be with us until one of us dies.

We have a plot at St Batholomew's Church in Longbenton with my mother and father, and that's where we will all go when our time comes. Jeni and Steph didn't want their brother to go into the cold ground on his own so he will go with one of us.

Leaving memories in the house is going to be the hardest thing I have done since Kenneth's funeral, but bricks and mortar can't hold what I keep in my heart. The thing is I'm ready for a time and place where Kenneth is not around every corner and in every room. I have my family to take me forward and we will take our memories of Kenneth along with us and build on them day by day.

One day Riley and Tai were getting out of the car and Tai started pointing and laughing. Then he said, 'Funny man showing his bum!' There was no one there. At least no one we could see. But Tai saw some-one and he spoke to them. Was it Uncle Kenneth telling him about the time he 'mooned' at the teacher? When that kind of thing happens I know Kenneth is not so far away after all!

My mother would have wanted me to maintain the strong family bond that she instilled in us and I suppose we keep Kenneth alive for Hannah, Riley and Tai because we talk about him often. We still have lots of photographs around to keep him with us and we still remember him in the things we do. Every 24 July we visit the National Memorial Arboretum near Lichfield to hold our own private ceremony at the beautiful Armed Forces Memorial. We stand at the spot where Kenneth's name is carved into the Portland stone and share our prayers and thoughts with him. On one of the visits Riley said: 'Is that Uncle Kenneth on the wall?' I said that it was, and that he died a soldier and was very brave. He knows that Kenneth is in Heaven now and I don't worry when he says he wants to go there and meet him. We all wish we could do that or have him back here for just a day.

Kenneth made it clear in his 'admin' letter that if he died he didn't want us to go out of our way for him. But we will visit the Arboretum every year for as long as we can and remember him and honour him. He's my son and he will always be part of our future and not just our past.

I could get very depressed if I spent too long thinking about Kenneth's death and, although I still have the odd time when it all gets too much for me, I don't think it's fair to let go and get lost in it all when I have so much to do and so much of the future to look forward to. Kenneth would have agreed with that. He loved children and he would have been Riley and Tai's favourite uncle without a shadow of a doubt. Kenneth was still a big kid at heart and the boys would have seen that right away. My son did a lot of growing up in Afghanistan. From the moment he heard that he had a baby daughter he gained an air of responsibility. If fate had granted him the chance, he would have made a lovely daddy.

Kenneth's daughter, Hannah, is a joy in our lives. I'm so sad that he didn't live to see her and hold her as he wanted to, but the lovely thing is, she knows all about him. And she knows he died a hero. She is such a beautiful little girl and as long as we have Hannah in our lives we have a part of Kenneth, and we see more of her daddy's sense of fun and mischief in her every day. She is part of a future that Kenneth would have enjoyed and we would have shared. That's where the joy and the sadness collide and I feel the loss so keenly for Hannah. We have all lost him and we all miss him. So very much.

Being an Army dog handler wasn't just a job for Kenneth; it was everything to him and it expressed a part of him. Every night I prayed to God to keep him safe. I don't know why that wasn't enough to save him. Maybe it was because I told him not to volunteer for anything, and then, on his last day before going on R and R, he requested to stay behind with Sasha so they could protect the men in the patrol. It was typical of Kenneth to do something like that and I'm so proud of him, but it shook my faith for quite a while. I could only reconcile myself with the thought that his death was for a reason: I'm just not sure what on earth that reason could be, and I'm not sure I will ever work it out.

For me, Kenneth will live on in my heart and in the hearts of everyone who knew and loved him. He is our hero forever. In that way he is still with us all the time, every day. It's such a strong feeling that sometimes I forget that he has gone – but then a knock at the door can bring it all back in an instant.

JANE

When Liam was killed in Afghan in 2011 my world stopped. As any mother with a son or daughter in the Armed Forces will tell you, it's a knock on the door you have to prepare yourself to expect from the moment they sign up, but a bigger part of you has to believe it will never happen, otherwise the fear of the moment will drive you mad. But that moment I had dreaded for six years found me.

Guilt is a terrible thing. You can't run from it and it will bolt you down, if you let it. Where Liam is concerned I still carry a fair old hump of guilt around with me. If he was here I'd just say: 'Liam, I'm sorry I sent you the wrong games for your Xbox. I'm sorry you never really had much space of your own at home. I'm sorry for all those bloomin' letters I kept sending while you were in Afghan and for anything I ever missed out of a parcel for you and Theo. I'm just sorry for anything I ever did wrong or you were unhappy about.' If I had the chance I would do it all right. And do you know what Liam would say to me: 'Chill out, Mum. Life is for living, not worrying!'

It was an attitude that made Liam one of the best people to be around. If I was worried about anything, he would find a way to stop me. He had a gift for reading situations and doing the right thing. Sometimes that was to listen, sometimes to make the person laugh

– whatever it took, really, because helping others mattered a great deal to him. Some would say Liam was cock-sure, others would say confident, but the performer in him was always there, he couldn't help it. The lovable rogue with the heart of gold – that's what I will always miss about Liam. He was fun to have around. And I think we all need at least one person in our lives that can make us feel that way.

Moving on in life without someone who made such a big impact on us every day is not easy, but I am very lucky. All the tangible reminders of Liam provide so much of what I need to pick me up when I fall into the dark times, where weakness and hopelessness wait to take me under. The very many letters of condolence I received after we lost Liam still feed my need to remember and value the contribution my son made, not just to my life, but to others' too. There are several that I dip into regularly but there is one that keeps me beyond tears and fills me with pride and hope every time. It's the now thinning and tattered bluey from Major (now Lieutenant Colonel) Alex Turner of the Irish Guards.

FOB Khar Nikah
22 March 2011
I write on the day – I gather – Liam is being buried. The close of a chapter none of us will ever forget and the passing of a friend to us all.

You have by now no doubt received many letters and messages of condolence. I hope that these have, at least, imparted how much Liam was loved and respected. Words can't salve wounds of the heart but I find them to be a worthwhile guide to reflection ... As Liam's Commander at the time of his death, there are things I hope you might appreciate hearing ...

There was so much that Liam – and of course Theo – brought to our lives.

My Company has really suffered from Improvised Explosive Devices on this tour. Eight strikes in all, resulting in many life-changing injuries. This spate hit our confidence extremely hard, especially since the devices in question are only getting harder to find. Then Liam arrived. It was like opening a window in a room where you've lain ill – flushing it with fresh air and sunlight. Theo charged around wagging his tail and snuffling around all the ditches and thickets that so intimidated us.

Liam beamed and chatted: he was so gregarious, almost cocky. He must have been scared himself (we all are) but did such a magnificent job of disguising it. As an officer, I'm familiar with the challenge in this.

The two of them brought a palpable sense of domesticity to our base. Liam would exercise

Theo in the mornings and throw his yellow ball.
On our shingled helicopter landing pad, they
might have been on Brighton beach! Liam was
always in command of brew area, making us
laugh and teasing his dog, like one of his mates.
At work and rest, those two carried us along.
How we miss them.

The Operation on which Liam was killed had
been planned – and resourced – meticulously.
Please know that I take my responsibilities to
heart and will surely carry the losses to my own
grave. We went over and over the plan. The
ambush was audacious and they paid for it with
dead and wounded of their own. I contend that
Liam was killed instantly – certainly he was
unconscious immediately – though we did
everything we could. My doctor was valiant, as
were all the boys around him. They broke cover
under fire to reach him. We never gave up. Doc
was in tears afterwards, such was his frustration
and sadness.

Liam and Theo were at the front – where he
always badgered me to send him. So he died for
us, and Theo soon after. 'Greater love hath no
man than to lay down his life for his friends.'
We will never forget Liam and I for one will
never set eyes on a Spaniel without thinking of
them both and what they did for us in those

weeks in Helmand. It will bring tears to my eyes.

We built a cross for them, and have put a photograph of them in the Memorial Gallery in the Forward Operating Base, so others will remember, too. On St Patrick's Day we gathered fresh green shamrock around the base of the cross. Theo would have tried to eat it!

But the real memorial will be in our hearts. There is no bond like comradeship, same as that of a parent to a child. I can only imagine your grief. We prayed for you at his memorial service in Khar Nikah and our continual prayers come with this letter.

Please be proud of your son. Liam was a truly courageous and generous soul. He came to help us and fate punished him. But in doing so a message was sent far and wide: example, sacrifice, selfless, spirit in the face of adversity. These are not just words but things men like Liam live by – and die for. Ignominious as death on a battlefield always is, Liam's nobility will outlast us all.

Yours ever

Alex

Letters of condolence came from far and wide and from those I had heard of and some I had not. Liam's death was announced in the House of Commons and letters came in from the Prime Minister and Alex Salmond, amongst many others. It was good to be reassured that my son's life had not been spent in vain, and believe me, kind words were not wasted on me.

Probably my proudest moment of all where Liam is concerned was to be told that he had been nominated for a gallantry award. His OC in Afghan, Major Caroline Emmett, had put him forward and he received a coveted Mention in Dispatches. How terribly sad that it was a posthumous award because Liam would have been over the moon to know that he was to be honoured in this way and formally recognised for the record number of 'finds' his dog Theo made in the space of just five months in theatre.

When I read the citation it made me cry ... for many, many reasons. To think of my son, '*demonstrating immense bravery and coolness under pressure ...*' It goes on, '*Liam accompanied Theo as the dog indicated on a horde of Pressure-Plate Improvised Explosive Devices (PPIEDs), batteries, improvised detonators and other items that, in the hands of the insurgents, were destined to kill or maim soldiers and civilians. Volunteering to take Theo further into the search area resulted in the discovery of more weapons and ammunition, RPGs and bomb making equipment.*'

What I thought was so special was that the citation not only commended Liam's skill as a handler but as a soldier when it said, '... *Tasker demonstrated incredible courage. His work in finding explosives, IEDs, arms and ammunition whilst under insurgent fire, undoubtedly saved lives.*'

I read it with a huge lump in my throat because I know Liam would have said: 'I was just doing my job, Mum.' But I still wish he had lived to read it for himself and receive the honour in person. At least he saw Theo receive his Para Wings. And that must have been my son's proudest moment.

Moving on is one thing but I never, ever want Liam Tasker's name to be forgotten. Fortunately, there are a lot of people who feel the same way. I knew that Liam's friends and colleagues in the RAVC will never let it happen or his old REME friends either, and it didn't take them very long to come up with a number of ideas for memorial sporting challenges – the Tri-Service Challenge for the Liam Tasker Trophy at SHAPE being just one of them. I can't thank all those young lads and lasses enough for everything they have done and are still doing to keep Liam alive in the thoughts of others and to help his family through the worst time possible.

When the rest of Liam's unit returned from Afghan his OC came up to Tayport with some of the lads to attend their own private service in the church where we held the funeral. They wanted to pay their respects at Liam's graveside and raise a glass of port – leaving a glass for their friend. Liam wouldn't have liked to be left out. It was all very emotional, but something they said they needed to do. Bless them. They are really very special people.

You really don't know how special individuals can be until you experience the bad times, and I've discovered – the hard way – that there are some very hard-working groups and charities out there ready to help, too. When you lose a loved one in war, a portal opens that you didn't even know existed. Sometimes they find you and sometimes you have to find them, but they are there. Out of the shadows strides a whole army of people who want to reach out to you and offer help of all kinds, and I have been extremely grateful for everything I've received and, most valuable of all, the new friends I have made.

SSAFA (the UK's oldest national military charity, formerly known as Soldiers, Sailors, Airmen and Families Association) came into my life by chance and at just the right time. The Army, through my assigned Family Liaison Officer, was doing all it could for me, and then someone mentioned SSAFA. Of course, having being connected with the military for so long I knew exactly what this wonderful charity was all about and aware of the invaluable support it provides to

Forces' and ex-Forces' personnel and their families. What didn't register straight away with me was that my family was now eligible to call on them for help. We had now entered the network of SSAFA friends and family and I knew that connection would give me access to the most valuable resource of all – other people who had been through exactly the same experience and knew how we felt.

Through the charity's Bereaved Families Support Group I met some wonderful mothers who were ready to share their coping strategies and help support me though my personal hell. From the first meeting in the October following Liam's death in March 2011, I knew that I was amongst good and wise friends. I felt humbled when I met the brave mothers whose soldier sons and daughters had taken their own lives as a result of PTSD (Post Traumatic Stress Disorder) and others whose lives had been changed beyond recognition by the loss of a limb. And there were plenty of cases like that. As one mother said, I suppose people forget that when you hear on the news that one soldier died when the vehicle he was travelling in was struck by an IED there's likely to be several other soldiers who are left with life-changing injuries. You can't be a soldier with one leg or one arm. Your career is over.

I was in awe of that group of mighty women, but ironically, when they met me, they said they felt guilty. Why? I had to ask them, because I didn't understand.

They said it was because their children lived and my child died. I asked them to please not feel like that at all because I can't imagine how Liam would have coped with losing a limb. All I know is that it would not have been easy for him – not for any of us. I'm not sure I would have dealt with the situation as well as those extraordinary women.

Through the bereaved mothers group I found understanding friends and a comfort zone that I needed to experience to believe existed. My children were offered the service, too, through the sibling support groups, and that made so much sense. Even though we had all experienced the same loss we were suffering in different ways and needed different levels of support. But there was one thing we all had in common: we realised that we were not alone and that everything we were feeling was perfectly normal.

Somehow I just needed someone to tell me I was going to survive this ordeal, and these other mothers were living proof that it was more than possible. I was welcomed into the SSAFA family and I'm still there today. I take part in the charity's fundraising events and I never hold back from telling people the value in getting help – from the right places.

Once the healing process began I found that I could turn my attention to some of the practical things that had been put to one side. Jimmy and the girls were very patient with me but I knew I had to listen to them and decide what we needed to do. We looked at those boxes of Liam's things and I remembered one of the mothers suggesting a new charity called Forces Support, founded by Bill McCance.

I didn't have to wait long for Forces Support to come up with a simple, practical solution to my problem. They built a garden shed that was dry, safe and secure, and just perfect for storing all of Liam's boxes. I didn't have to worry about them any more – they could come out of my brother's garage and come home at last. It seemed to me that the boxes had become a symbol of my guilt – that I couldn't accommodate Liam's belongings in the house. They were a reminder that he had gone, and only a few boxes filled with bits and pieces from a career, loved and lived, remained. Now, at least, I know they are safe, but I don't think I will ever be able to open them – as long as I live.

There are many lasting tributes that come in so many forms: letters, photographs, paintings, DVDs, medals (Liam's and Theo's) that will ensure that my son and his beloved dog will never be forgotten. Ian, my eldest son, designed his own tribute to his little brother – a sepia tattoo on his back depicting Liam and Theo together. Liam was going to add to his own tattoo collection when he returned from his tour; it was going to be those words: Each day is a gift, not a given right. They are words we, as a family, will never forget.

A few months after Liam's funeral I started to make enquiries to get Liam's name up on the War Memorial in Tayport. I was one proud mamma when on 1 March 2012 Liam's name went up on the wall and we had a re-dedication service. Another proud but emotional day – and God, we've had a few of them – was when Liam's name appeared on the Armed Forces Memorial at the National Memorial Arboretum in Staffordshire. It's so sad to see all those names up there. I now know many of the mums and dads personally so to me they are more than names etched in Portland stone.

In June 2015 we returned to the Arboretum for the unveiling of the Bastion Wall. Prince Harry's speech was delivered as if he wanted to speak to each person there, to each connection with the 453 killed in Afghanistan. We saw Liam's name – the 358th British soldier to be killed out there – and as I stood in the sunshine I remember thinking, please let him be the last so no other family goes through what I'm going through.

Liam was everything I could want in a son and everything the Army could want in a soldier. I have lost my father and my grandmother but I can tell you, with all certainty, nothing compares with the pain of losing your child. It is still a huge sadness that weighs heavy on time and thought every day from the moment I wake up and, to some degree, until bedtime. The strange thing is I feel its power lessening. After the usual feelings when I wake up of 'Was that real or was it a nightmare?' I can sometimes go through the whole morning at work before I feel that sensation of deep loss again. Whenever that happens I get upset and feel guilty for the rest of the day, even though I accept that it's all part of the grieving process.

I'm starting to rationalise that just because thoughts of Liam no longer dominate my waking and sleeping hours I've not stopped loving him. All I've done is put things into perspective and put the living first. When my daughter Laura gave birth to her first child in 2014, I was so excited I thought I was going to burst. But I couldn't hold off the massive surge of sadness that came over me the moment I realised that the wee bairn – Harry Liam – would never know his namesake. And Liam would have spoilt him so much and made such a fuss of him. It's just so sad they will never know each other.

Moving on, I've learned, means not living with the trappings of that person all around you but keeping some things close and leaving others out of sight. It works for me, at least. Sometimes I delve into the box of letters and choose one to read just to bring Liam back to me, and it works even if it is just for a few moments. I still wonder how he put up with all the drivel I shared with him every day he was out there fighting the Taliban!

In one letter I told him that I'd had a new washing machine and how the delivery guy had covered the hall carpet in muddy footprints, forcing me to spend the entire afternoon cleaning up. I can tell you right now I would give anything to see the tread of Liam's boots on that hall carpet. Just once more. Just for a second. I would trace the outline of his footprint with my hands – and wonder, what if …?

To lose Liam and Theo at the same time was right for them. I believe that somewhere out there they are running together. Sometimes I visualise them running in a field but other times they are out in the desert working side by side searching for bombs and explosives and keeping everyone safe. When I close my eyes they are always smiling.

Epilogue

The Fallen

by Director Army Veterinary and Remount Services
Colonel Douglas Macdonald QHVS

'Perhaps there may be a temptation for those
who have never come across RAVC dog handlers
to assume they are a softer type of soldier, purely
because their role involves animals. However, all
who have served alongside them in theatre will
know the truth and the truth is that these men
and women have huge reservoirs of courage
matched by a deep trust, all of which they place
in their dog's abilities. And they do this as they
serve at the sharp and pointy end of the front
line, often going out front to ensure the safety of
others.'

Rev Paul Gallucci,
Artillery Group and Dog Unit Chaplain,
Camp Bastion, Afghanistan, 2008

This book has explored the lives and duties of two exceptional Royal Army Veterinary Corps dog handlers: Lance Corporals Kenneth Rowe and Liam Tasker, along with their dogs Sasha and Theo. The book also bravely examined the effect their deaths had on their families and particularly on their mothers. At times I felt that the passages from those proud but grief-stricken mothers were written not with ink, but with tears. Their words moved me, and I am sure that every reader will have felt the same deep sympathy and admiration for Lyn Rowe and Jane Duffy over how they came to terms with the death of their sons.

As a Veterinary Officer in the Corps it has been my honour and privilege to witness, many times over, the loyalty and dedication shown by handlers and their dogs for each other; and when reading this book I very clearly remembered the moments when the death of a soldier and their dog has touched my professional and personal life. The first was in May 1986 when Corporal Brian Brown QGM serving with 3 UDR (Ulster Defence Regiment) was killed in an explosion alongside his dog Oliver. As the Veterinary Officer for the Army Dog Unit in Northern Ireland I was required to conduct the necropsy on Oliver as evidence for the police. The second and third occasions happened when I was in command of the Defence Animal Centre, where our animals and handlers in Defence are given their first training. In July 2008 we heard the sad news that Kenneth Rowe and Sasha had been killed, and then again in March 2011 when Liam Tasker was killed, and later that same day we learned of the death of his beloved dog, Theo. Lance Corporal Kenneth Rowe and his dog Sasha and Lance Corporal Liam Tasker and his dog Theo are two examples of the best there can be in RAVC dog-and-handler teams. Theirs was a unique bond created in the training environment but forged in the heat of battle. The losses hit the men and women of the Royal Army Veterinary Corps hard. Anyone who was serving at those times will remember where they were and what they were doing when the dreadful news broke.

The conflict in Afghanistan called for all of our detection dogs to be of the highest calibre. Each one had to have the intelligence, athleticism and aptitude to be trained to detect the weapons created by the Taliban. The devices were designed to inflict maximum devastation on our troops and the civilian population, and the threat was ever present and evolving. This meant that our dog teams were always on high alert and in constant demand. Sasha and Theo were both trained to give their best in an extremely challenging environment, and both were known and recognised for their drive and ability to detect weapons and explosives. In a conflict in which the risk of injury or death was always present, the dogs gave Kenneth and Liam confidence and comradeship in equal measure. Similarly the dogs were given succour, support, encouragement and love from their handlers. Without doubt their team-work, and their complementary skills and gifts, saved the lives and limbs of many soldiers and civilians in Afghanistan. And all of the time neither the dog nor the handler were ever alone; they were constant comrades doing the best they could in a bad place.

It was after the First World War, on 27 November 1918, that His Royal Highness King George V conferred the title 'Royal' on the Army Veterinary Corps in recognition of its work caring for the horses, mules, camels, pigeons and dogs on the battlefields of Europe and the Middle East. Since then the dogs and handlers of the RAVC have been a constant element in the Allied force: the Second World War cemented the role of the military working dog in conflict, and this was taken forward to conflicts in Korea and Malaya and then in larger numbers during the British Army presence in Northern Ireland, Bosnia (1995–2005), Kosovo (1999–2003), Iraq (2003–2009) and then Afghanistan (2003–2014).

'It is not unreasonable to say that the War Dog is probably more firmly established as part of the armed forces than ever before. Despite the breath-taking advances in modern armaments there will always be scope for the talents of trained dogs, no matter where the Army is called upon to operate. Nothing that man has invented, or is likely to invent in the foreseeable future, can replace these qualities which have made the dog such an outstanding member of the animal kingdom and the devoted servant of man.'

Brigadier George Young, MBE,
Director of the Army Veterinary
and Remount Services, 1953

'The capability they [military working dogs] bring to the fight cannot be replicated by man or machine. By all measures of performance their yield outperforms any asset we have in our inventory. Our Army (and military) would be remiss if we failed to invest more in this incredibly valuable resource.'

General David H. Petraeus, 2010

While almost sixty years span the above quotes they are as relevant today as when they were first written. The dogs and handlers of 1 Military Working Dog Regiment (Royal Army Veterinary Corps) are in a constant state of readiness to supply the Defence Army with the relevant dogs to do whatever job is required of them at home and overseas.

Over the last decade the RAVC dog handler, man and woman, has emerged as an essential element of military capability, one that continues to evolve and improve to meet new threats at home and overseas. Our detection dogs, with their skilled and dedicated handlers, save life and limb wherever they serve, and as such they are revered by all as a unique and effective fighting force in all operations. Our handlers and their dogs exemplify the professionalism and courage of all those who serve our country and we are justly proud of them; and they do all of this under the watchful and caring eye of the Corps' Colonel in Chief, Her Royal Highness the Princess Royal.

Behind every man or woman who joins the Armed Forces there is a family who inevitably, and invisibly, serves too in their own way. To those who choose to 'Follow the Drum' their family can be their touchstone of normality and a welcome reminder of home. To the family of a dog soldier the dog can be silent comforter and a reassurance that, whatever happens, whatever the battle brings to bear, their loved one will not die alone. This has clearly been a great comfort to the families of Kenneth and Liam; especially to their mothers.

In a dog handler's career there will be many dogs but there will always be one dog that steals your heart. For

THE FALLEN

the warrior who has the enviable privilege of serving alongside a war dog there is a certainty that they will care, share and look out for each other. When one is hurt, the other will be there to comfort them. And when the world looks hostile or lonely they are half of an inseparable partnership that no one – and no event, not even death – can break.

This is something that Kenneth Rowe's and Liam Tasker's families know well. They were, and will always be remembered as, two young men driven by dedication to their job and loyalty to their comrades and their country. Their loss to the Corps still resonates. Good people, good sons, good soldiers. They made their parents proud and a nation thankful for their sacrifice. For their service to the Corps, their sovereign and their country we will remember them. For their sense of duty and their ultimate sacrifice we know that we are, forever, in the presence of heroes.

Director Army Veterinary and Remount Services
Colonel Douglas Macdonald QHVS

ROLL OF HONOUR – FOR THE FALLEN IN THE FACE OF THE ENEMY

Greater love hath no man than this, that a man lay down his life for his friends.

John, 15:13

Cpl Bryan Criddle BEM joined the Poineer Corps at the age of 17 and later transferred to the RAVC to become a dog trainer. On 6 July 1973 he was awarded the British Empire Medal in recognition of his service in Northern Ireland. Just 12 days later he was on patrol searching an open area with the 16/5 Lancers near Clogher, County Tyrone, in the heart of 'bandit country', when his search dog Jason indicated on a milk churn. Having warned fellow troops to stay clear Corporal Criddle was then caught in a blast as the five bombs, buried in a horseshoe formation, were detonated remotely by IRA terrorists watching from over the border. Corporal Criddle died four days later in Musgrave Park Hospital as a result of severe head injuries. He left a wife, Julia, and daughter, Sarah aged three, and twin boys, Gary and Glenn aged 10 months.

Jason was blown 30 feet into the air in the blast but survived with minor injuries. Jason, who had recently been awarded his 'wings' for completing 1,000 flying hours in helicopters moving between the garrison and the border to carry out his duties, stood guard over his injured master on the ground.

Cpl Brian Brown QGM from Ballynahinch was a member of 3 UDR (Ulster Defence Regiment) and had been awarded the Queen's Gallantry Medal for his service in Northern Ireland. He lost his life on 28 May 1986 when a bomb exploded at a garage in Kilkeel. He left a wife and four children. Oliver, his search dog, was also killed in the blast. The ashes of the faithful Yellow Labrador were buried with his master.

Cpl Derek Hayes of the Royal Pioneer Corps died with his Army search dog, Ben, when an IRA booby trap bomb exploded. Cpl Hayes and Ben were on patrol in Crossmaglen when they were asked to investigate a partly hidden box in a ditch, but as they approached the device exploded, killing them both. Corporal Hayes was 28 years old and married with a young child. The ashes of his faithful Yellow Labrador, Ben, were buried alongside the soldier.

Corporal Terry O'Neill of the Royal Regiment of Fusiliers and his fellow dog handler Corporal Darren 'Swifty' Swift were in the rear exercise area of the Army barracks at North Howard Street Mill in Belfast on 25 May 1991 when an IRA terrorist hurled a 'coffee-jar' bomb (containing Semtex, a detonator and 'shipyard confetti' – nuts, bolts, rivets, screws and nails) from the fire escape of the snooker hall, directly above the handlers. The homemade bomb landed at the soldiers' feet, killing Geordie instantly and taking Swifty's legs – and a finger – clean away. Their dogs, Blue and Troy, somehow survived the blast but needed veterinary care for their injuries.

That sunny Saturday afternoon of the Bank Holiday weekend one life was taken and the other changed forever in one brief, brutal and deliberate act of violence. Corporal O'Neill was due to retire from the Army in six months after a career spanning 22 years. He was the last Army Dog Unit Northern Ireland handler to die in The Troubles.

Note: This is not a definitive list of all who have lost their lives whilst serving Queen and Country during The Troubles in Northern Ireland during Operation Banner. For the purposes of the book we have listed the handlers and dogs who were killed or injured as a result of an act of terrorism or enemy action alongside their soldier dogs.

After the death of Cpl Bryan Criddle BEM in July 1973 the RAVC, as a small, specialist Corps, did not lose another dog and handler in enemy action until the deaths of LCpl Kenneth Rowe and Sasha in Afghanistan in July 2008. When the RAVC lost LCpl Liam Tasker and Theo in March 2011 it confirmed, if anyone had ever doubted it, that the dog handlers of the RAVC and throughout the Armed Forces remain very much on the front line. In the fight against terrorism the dog soldiers are recognised and well respected for their battle-winning capability – a force to face and ultimately assist in defeating the enemy.

Warriors all.

THE RED PAW ASSOCIATION

The Red Paw Association remains a badge of honour worn with great pride by both serving and veteran dog handlers. All soldier dogs before and after the institution of the Badge have set their bloodied paws on the ground where good has fought many battles against evil at home and overseas. Many dogs lost their lives in The Troubles in Northern Ireland and in their sacrifice saved many human lives. In all other conflicts after the Second World War – Korea, Northern Ireland, the Falklands, Bosnia, Iraq and Afghanistan, they will be forever recognised for their loyalty, dedication and unstinting devotion.

To those who served and protected and those who sacrificed all – we salute you.

THE RAVC COLLECT

O God who didst create man in thine own
   image,
And gavest him dominion over every living
   thing,
Give wisdom and grace, we pray thee, to thy
   servants of the Royal Army Veterinary Corps
That we may guard these thy creatures
   committed to our care
Against disease and suffering
And promote their health and usefulness:
And may ever declare both by word and
   example
That the merciful man is kind to his beast,
For His sake, who has told us that one sparrow
   is forgotten before thee,
Jesus Christ our merciful redeemer.
Amen.